Making

Victoria Butler-Cole KC of 39 Essex Chambers works in the fields of health and social care law, across a range of areas including community care, regulatory and disciplinary law, judicial review, mental health, mental capacity, best interests and human rights claims. She is enthusiastic about explaining the law to non-lawyers so that people are better able to understand their obligations and assert their rights.

Steve Broach KC of 39 Essex Chambers is a public lawyer with particular expertise in health, education and social care and disability and children's rights cases. He is a discrimination specialist and is also regularly instructed in civil claims raising human rights and discrimination issues. Steve took Silk in 2024. Prior to this, he was frequently instructed as 'leading junior' in high profile judicial review cases, including challenges to central government policies and decisions. Steve is passionate about improving the quality of decision-making, particularly where decisions affect disadvantaged groups, and frequently provides training to local government and NHS bodies on legal issues.

The Legal Action Group is a national, independent charity which campaigns for equal access to justice for all members of society.

Legal Action Group:

- Strengthens the voice of people and communities denied access to justice
- Supports frontline charities, lawyers and advisers to deliver access to justice
- Influences law and policy to improve access to justice and create a fair legal system for all.

Making Lawful Decisions

A guide for decision-makers on acting within the law

FIRST EDITION

Victoria Butler-Cole KC
Steve Broach KC

LAG Legal Action Group
2024

This edition published in Great Britain 2024
by LAG Education and Service Trust Limited
Gatehouse Chambers, 1 Lady Hale Gate, London WC1X 8BS
www.lag.org.uk

British Library Cataloguing in Publication Data
A CIP catalogue record for this book is available from the British Library.

FSC www.fsc.org MIX Board | Supporting responsible forestry FSC® C020438

This book has been produced using Forest Stewardship Council (FSC) certified paper. The wood used to produce FSC certified products with a 'Mixed Sources' label comes from FSC certified well-managed forests, controlled sources and/or recycled material.

print 978-1-913648-62-6
ebook 978-1-913648-63-3
bundle (print and ebook) 978-1-913648-64-0

Typeset by Refinecatch Limited, Bungay, Suffolk
Printed in Great Britain by Hobbs the Printers, Totton, Hampshire

Contents

Foreword

A hundred years ago, in 1924, a schoolteacher was dismissed by the local education authority on the ground that she had got married: *Short v Poole Corp* [1926] Ch 66, CA. The Court of Appeal held that the local authority had acted lawfully within its powers. It would have been different if it had dismissed a teacher for having red hair, but it was not unreasonable to dismiss her because she had got married. There was nothing that Mrs Short could do as a matter of law to complain about her dismissal. In the century since then, the law has changed beyond all recognition. The common law has developed, especially since the 1960s, with principles of judicial review or what we now call 'public law' increasingly prominent. And parliament has enacted legislation such as the Sex Discrimination Act 1975 (which has now been replaced by the Equality Act 2010) and the Human Rights Act 1998.

Anyone who reads a newspaper or looks at social media will have come across phrases such as 'judicial review', 'the GDPR', 'protected characteristics', etc. But the law in this area can be confusing, especially for people who are not themselves lawyers. It is very important that decision-makers and others should have access to a readable introduction to the legal duties and processes which are expected of decision-makers in a variety of contexts, not all of which are governed by public law. The authors of this book, Victoria Butler-Cole KC and Steve Broach KC, are to be congratulated for providing that introduction. It is written in a practical way, using helpful checklists for decision-makers.

This book also has the advantage that it brings together various different parts of the law which are sometimes treated as specialist areas, for example, public law and discrimination law. In the real world, people do not bring problems with neat legal labels attached to them. It is important, not only for lay people but also for their legal advisers, to appreciate that there may be more than one angle from which a problem needs to be looked at. Data protection principles may be relevant as well as equality principles and human rights principles. And it is very important that silos should not develop in different types of decision-making. Sometimes, people who specialise in prison work need to know what the law has said in a very different context, for example, to do with tax. There may be relevant legal principles which need to be considered even though they are well outside a person's specialist area of decision-making. This book will help people to keep an eye on that bigger picture.

The Rt Hon Lord Justice Singh

Authors' note

This book is concerned with the requirements for lawful decision-making. We include within this concept both decisions made by individuals and those made by panels or other quasi-judicial bodies. Although many of the legal requirements discussed in the book are imposed by public law, we hope that it will prove useful for both public and private sector decision-makers, and the many decision-makers working in the grey areas in between. We anticipate that private sector decision-makers will want to ensure that their decisions meet the standards imposed by public law, even where this is not strictly required.

At its essence, this book is about fairness. The law does not purport to tell decision-makers *what* to decide. The law is primarily concerned with *how* decisions are made – so that the decision-maker considers all the relevant information and discounts irrelevant information, is not biased against one party or in favour of another, allows parties to make representations in writing or orally where this is required, and so on.

Many of these principles stem from the common law and are well established. The book also considers two areas where the obligations arise from statute and have been imposed more recently – the need to comply with the non-discrimination principles in the Equality Act (EA) 2010 and the human rights standards in the European Convention on Human Rights, given effect through the Human Rights Act (HRA) 1998. Again, although the book looks at who precisely must comply with both the EA 2010 and the HRA 1998 in making decisions, we anticipate that even those decision-makers who are not strictly required to avoid discrimination (a very small number) or to respect human rights (a somewhat larger number), will want to do so.

The book follows the typical structure of decision-making, taking into account the potential need for a hearing prior to the decision being made and the specific requirements imposed in that context. It is intended to be read by the widest possible pool of decision-makers, in particular those with no legal training, and so does not delve into the specific requirements of decision-making in particular sectors or areas – although some points are illustrated by way of examples from the case-law.

We have used the following terminology:

- Decision-maker: the individual, group or panel making a decision.
- Party or person: anyone directly affected by the decision.

Although the book is primarily addressed to decision-makers, we also hope it will prove useful to those who are aggrieved by a decision or decisions and are considering a complaint or legal challenge. To that end, and also to inform decision-makers, we have included a section on remedies where the lawfulness of a decision is put in question.

We are very grateful to all the contributors who have shared their expertise in supporting and challenging lawful decision-making. We would also be grateful for feedback from users of this book, including any corrections and/or requests for further issues to be addressed in future editions. Please send any feedback to Steve Broach at Steve.Broach@39essex.com.

Victoria Butler-Cole KC
Steve Broach KC
39 Essex Chambers
July 2024

List of contributors

Jack Anderson (39 Essex Chambers) – Hearings chapter
Katherine Barnes (39 Essex Chambers) – Remedies chapter and rationality section
Adam Boukraa (39 Essex Chambers) – Human Rights Act chapter and legitimate expectation section
Stephanie David (39 Essex Chambers) – Equality Act chapter
Michael Etienne (Garden Court Chambers) – Equality Act chapter and Glossary
David Hopkins (39 Essex Chambers) – Hearings chapter
Ruth Keating (39 Essex Chambers) – Preparation chapter
Alex Littlewood (Monckton Chambers) – improper motive and relevant considerations sections
Ciar McAndrew (Monckton Chambers) – reasons section
Imogen Proud (Monckton Chambers) – legitimate expectation section
Rachel Sullivan (39 Essex Chambers) – rationality section
Gethin Thomas (39 Essex Chambers) – Preparation chapter

Table of cases

Table of statutes

Table of statutory instruments

Table of EU and international instruments

European Convention on the Protection of Human Rights and Fundamental Freedoms 1951 (ECHR)	4.85, 5.34, 6.1, 6.2, 6.3, 6.4, 6.13, 6.14, 6.15, 6.16, 6.17, 6.18, 6.19, 6.20–6.22, 6.23–6.63, 6.65, 6.66, 6.69, 6.70, 6.71, 7.37
Art 2	6.20
Art 3	6.20, 6.32
Art 4	6.20
Art 5	6.20
Art 6	2.3, 6.20, 6.34–6.45
Art 6(1)	6.38, 6.41
Art 7	6.20
Art 8	6.20, 6.27, 6.46–6.48, 6.52, 6.55, 6.58
Art 8(2)	6.48
Art 9	5.31, 6.20, 6.49–6.52
Art 9(2)	6.52
Art 10	6.20, 6.53–6.55
Art 10(2)	6.55
Art 11	6.20
Art 12	6.20
Art 14	4.61, 5.10, 5.14, 6.11, 6.20, 6.56–6.60
Art 16	6.20
Art 17	6.20
Art 18	6.20
Art 41	6.71
Protocol 1 Art 1	6.20, 6.61–6.63
Protocol 1 Art 2	6.20
Protocol 1 Art 3	6.20
Protocol 13 Art 1	6.20
Regulation (EU) 2016/679 of the European Parliament and of the Council of 27 April 2016 on the protection of natural persons with regard to the processing of personal data and on the free movement of such data, and repealing Directive 95/46/EC (General Data Protection Regulation, GDPR)	2.41, 2.46, 2.47–2.57, 2.58–2.62

Glossary

Adjournment Delaying or postponing a hearing or decision to a later date.

Appeal A challenge to an earlier decision. Often used in relation to a decision by a court or tribunal but can also be used to describe a challenge to a decision by an administrative decision-maker, if there is a higher level of consideration (eg an appeal panel).

Burden of proof The responsibility for convincing a court or tribunal about a fact or issue that is required before a legal dispute can be resolved. See also *Standard of proof* and *Tribunal*.

Common law Legal rules, practices or procedures which derive from decisions by courts taken over time rather than from legislation.

Cross-examination The process where a witness is questioned by a representative of a party whose case the witness does not support, or by an unrepresented party themself.

Disclosure The process of providing the other parties to a decision with the information and documents you have that are relevant to that decision.

Evidence The information that is given to a decision-maker to use when making their decision. This could be information in a document, photo or video, or information given to a decision-maker orally during a hearing.

Examination The process of questioning a witness by a representative for a party, or by an unrepresented party themself. Where the witness is supportive of the party whose representative is

	asking the questions, this is usually known as 'examination in chief'.
Human rights	Legal principles, usually found in international agreements (Conventions), that set out rights which some or all people enjoy. For example, the European Convention on Human Rights applies to every person in the geographical area to which it applies, whereas the UN Convention on the Rights of the Child applies to persons under the age of 18.
Legislation	Legal rules contained within laws passed by a legislative body, usually a parliament. Often, broadly taking two forms: (i) primary legislation, eg Acts of a parliament that take effect after they have gone through all stages of parliamentary scrutiny; and (ii) secondary legislation, eg statutory instruments, which are created by the executive (government) without requiring full legislative scrutiny. See also *Statutory*.
Natural justice	The essential, basic requirements for a decision-making process to be considered to have been 'fair'. These are requirements that have been recognised by judges over many decades but are often described as being instinctive or intuitive. Invariably, it requires a person to be given an opportunity to be heard about a decision that affects them before it is taken, based on the same information available to the decision-maker, by a decision-maker who is not biased.
Non-statutory	A reference to a power or obligation to do something or refrain from doing something that is not set out in parliamentary legislation but comes from a different legal source, such as decisions by senior courts or guidance produced by government departments or statutory bodies.
Notice	Information that a decision is being considered or has been taken with some explanation of the reasons for it.
Privilege	Information is privileged if it is private and confidential between you and your legal representative. Not all information that you share with your legal representative will be subject

to privilege. Broadly speaking, communication with your legal representative for the purpose of getting legal advice or as part of litigation will be privileged. This means that it cannot be shared with other people unless you decide that you want it to be shared.

Proportionate — Proportionality is a legal standard which has four essential elements:

(1) that the decision furthers a legitimate aim;
(2) that the measure being decided on is rationally connected to that aim;
(3) that the measure being decided on is the least intrusive measure that is capable of achieving the legitimate aim; and
(4) that the measure being decided on strikes a fair balance between the rights of persons who will or may be negatively affected by it and any wider interests.

A decision will be proportionate if it meets all four stages of this test.

Reconsider — Where a decision-maker thinks again about their decision, perhaps because they recognise that the process by which it was taken was unfair, or because new information has come to light and the relevant rules allow that information to be taken into account.

Remedy — What a body such as a court or tribunal can do to put things right if the decision-maker has made a mistake. For example, a common remedy granted by the Administrative Court in an application for judicial review is a 'quashing order', which requires the decision-maker to take the decision again.

Representation — Where a party engages another person to act for them and put their case to the decision-maker. Representatives can be, but often do not need to be, lawyers.

Standard of proof — The level of confidence that a decision-maker must have in order to decide whether or not a particular event occurred and what the outcome of the case should be. Normally, unless the case is in a criminal court, the standard of proof will

	be 'on the balance of probabilities'. In criminal cases, the decision-maker (judge or jury) must be 'sure' that the relevant events happened.
Statutory	Something that is set out in laws passed by a parliament, such as a power or duty to do something or not do something. That may be the UK Parliament at Westminster or one of the devolved parliaments, such as the Welsh Parliament. For example, a 'statutory duty' to make reasonable adjustments for a disabled person.
Tribunal	A body established by law which has powers to resolve legal disputes between parties; similar to, but often less formal than, a court.
Witness	A person who provides information to a decision-maker based on their own experience of an event or issue. When that person provides information to a court or tribunal based solely on the fact that they have specialist knowledge or experience of an issue, that person may be described as an 'expert' witness.

CHAPTER 1

Checklist

1.1 This checklist is a summary of the matters that decision-makers need to consider in helping to ensure they make lawful decisions. Running through the checklist may be a useful starting point before steps are taken towards making a decision. It will also be relevant to those who are affected by decisions and want to see 'at a glance' if the decision taken in their case has been taken lawfully. More detail on the points included in the checklist is given in subsequent chapters of this book.

Checklist

(1) What are your powers?

- (a) Are you familiar with all the relevant legislation, codes of practice, other statutory or non-statutory guidance, policies or protocols governing your decision-making processes and powers?
- (b) What type of issues are you authorised to determine?
- (c) Are there any issues that you are not authorised to determine?
- (d) Are there any procedural rules that you must follow, whether set down in writing or based on past practice?
- (e) What is the test that has to be applied when making your decision?
- (f) Are the parties aware of all the above matters?

(2) Are there any problems with bias or conflicts of interest?

- (a) Does anyone involved in making the decision have a direct interest in the outcome?
- (b) Does anyone involved in making the decision have an indirect interest in the outcome?
- (c) Does anyone involved in making the decision have a prior relationship with one of the parties, or a body to which that party is connected?
- (d) Have there already been any discussions between the decision-maker and any of the parties or people closely related to them which are not known to the other parties?

(3) What is/are the question(s) that you have to decide?

- (a) Are there any preliminary issues or disagreements, for example, about procedures or your powers, that need to be resolved before you determine the main issue(s)?
- (b) Are the questions and the possible outcomes clear and understood by the decision-maker and the parties?

- (c) Which party has the burden of proof in demonstrating that a particular decision should be made?
- (d) What is the standard of proof that has to be satisfied – is it a test of 'the balance of probabilities' (which means that you are more than 50% satisfied), or 'beyond reasonable doubt' (which is a higher threshold and means being sufficiently certain that you are sure)?

(4) What evidence will you need to make your decision?

- (a) Do you have all the information you need?
- (b) Will you need to hear oral evidence from any person?
- (c) Do you have copies of any documents or correspondence that a party wants to rely on?
- (d) If one side is being given an opportunity to provide information or argument, has the same opportunity been given to the other side?
- (e) If another person or body has already made a decision about the same issue, do you have the evidence they relied on? Are you permitted or required to consider it, or their conclusions?

(5) What procedures should you follow?

- (a) Has everyone who should have had an opportunity to contribute to the decision been consulted?
- (b) Have all sides had a fair opportunity and sufficient time to set out their position and make their arguments?
- (c) If there is a hearing, have you thought about whether it should be in private or in public, or a mixture? Will the media and/or other interested persons be allowed to attend?
- (d) Are the parties permitted to have legal representation at any hearing or to make written submissions? Have all sides had access to such legal advice or support as they may be entitled to?
- (e) If there will be oral evidence from witnesses, who will be allowed to ask them questions? How will the process of questioning work? What order will the witnesses give evidence in? Will they be present while other people are giving evidence?
- (f) Where an allegation has been made about a person or a group of people, have they had a fair opportunity to consider the allegation and respond to it? This includes

making sure they have seen documents or other information relating to the allegation.

(g) What special arrangements might be needed for the parties, for example, translation and interpreting services for those with English as a second language, or support for disabled people such as 'easy read' materials or the appointment of an advocate?

(h) Have you ensured that you are complying fully with your data protection obligations in relation to the processing of personal information and sensitive personal information as part of the decision-making?

(6) How will you explain your decision?

(a) Do you have any specific duty to give reasons for your decision in a particular way or within a particular timeframe, for example, in accordance with a requirement of legislation or a code of practice?

(b) Have you identified the decision you are making and, if appropriate, explained what burden of proof and standard of proof apply?

(c) Are you sure you have done enough to familiarise yourself with all the relevant information?

(d) Have you identified the evidence and information relied on by both sides and summarised it?

(e) If there is evidence or information you disagree with or do not accept, have you explained why?

(f) If you have held an oral hearing and heard evidence from witnesses, what is your impression of each witness in terms of their reliability and credibility? Why?

(g) What factual findings are you making?

(h) Have you identified and set out the arguments being made by each side and explained why you do or do not agree with them?

(i) Do your reasons refer back to any policy, case-law or other guidance that you are required to take into account? Do they explain how you have applied that guidance rather than just stating what the guidance says and then stating your decision?

(j) Have you checked that you have taken into account all relevant considerations including any contained in law or guidance?

- (k) Have you checked that you have not taken into account any irrelevant considerations?
- (l) Have you set out your decision in writing and in a form that the affected parties can understand?

(7) What if your decision is challenged?

- (a) If you have an appeal process, has each party been told how to access it?
- (b) Are there clear rules about how appeals will be dealt with? Will there be a rehearing or a review?
- (c) For less formal decisions, is there a complaints process and does each party know about it and how to access it?
- (d) For decisions by public bodies, does the aggrieved party know that they can seek to challenge the decision by way of an application for judicial review?

CHAPTER 2

Preparation

continued

2.1 This chapter sets out the preliminary issues that decision-makers should consider when preparing to make a decision.

Should there be a hearing?

2.2 All decision-makers must come to a decision in a procedurally fair way. In the interests of fairness, it may be that affected parties need to be given the opportunity to make representations and/or that an oral hearing should be held – this means a hearing where the parties are 'present' (whether in person, by video link or, much less desirably, by phone) and can give evidence and make submissions to the decision-maker. This section deals with the circumstances where an oral hearing should take place and how parties can be involved where there is no oral hearing.

2.3 Importantly, a fair 'hearing' does not mean that there must always be an opportunity to be heard orally. Neither the principles of natural justice nor Article 6 of the European Convention on Human Rights demands that there be an oral hearing in every case.[1] Those affected by a decision are entitled to an oral hearing where fairness requires that there should be such a hearing. The general rule is that those impacted by a decision ought to be able to participate in the procedure by which the decision is made, provided they have something to say which is relevant to the decision to be taken.[2] But whether fairness requires an oral hearing will depend on all the circumstances of the individual case.[3]

2.4 A party must be afforded an oral hearing if the relevant procedural rules provide for such an entitlement. It is more likely that an oral hearing will be appropriate where there are factual disputes, but the presence of a factual dispute does not mean an oral hearing must be held.[4]

2.5 Some statutory tribunals, inquiries and other bodies are required by legislation to conduct oral hearings. If an oral hearing is required but is not held, this will usually result in the decision being invalid. Administrative convenience should not override the need for an oral

1 *Foster v Secretary of State for Justice* [2015] EWCA Civ 281 at [35]–[39].

2 *Osborn v Parole Board* [2013] UKSC 61 at [68].

3 *R (Calland) v Financial Ombudsman Service Ltd* [2013] EWHC 1327 (Admin) at [110].

4 *R (Calland) v Financial Ombudsman Service Ltd* [2013] EWHC 1327 (Admin) at [110].

hearing.[5] Where there is doubt as to whether an oral hearing is needed, the presumption should be in favour of an oral hearing taking place.[6]

2.6 The right to an oral hearing does not necessarily equate with the right to be personally present at the hearing (where the case is being conducted by a representative).[7]

2.7 A more detailed analysis of the requirements for a fair oral hearing is provided in chapter 3.

2.8 Even where there is no oral hearing, those with a stake in the decision should be informed of any adverse submissions or evidence and be given the opportunity to reply.[8]

2.9 What will be sufficient in terms of involvement of parties is a question of fairness, to be measured against all the circumstances. However, it may be the case that the opportunity to make written representations is all that fairness requires in particular circumstances.[9]

Consultation

2.10 This section outlines when a duty to consult will arise, and the legal requirements for fair consultation in circumstances where a decision-maker is under a duty to consult before making their decision, and/or is not under a duty but chooses to consult anyway.[10] One key

5 In *R v Department of Health ex p Gandhi* [1991] 1 WLR 1053, DC at 1063 the court emphasised that 'administrative convenience should not be allowed to override the exigencies of a particular case. An oral hearing should be held where, in all the circumstances, the issues cannot fairly be resolved otherwise'.

6 *R (Riley) v Governor of Frankland Prison* [2009] EWHC 3598 (Admin).

7 *R v Secretary of State for the Home Department ex p Wynne* [1992] QB 406, CA.

8 In *R v Huntingdon DC ex p Cowan* [1984] 1 WLR 501, DC the court held that when dealing with an application for an entertainments licence under Local Government (Miscellaneous Provisions) Act 1982 Part I a local authority was under a duty to inform the applicant of the substance of any objections to the licence being granted and to give the applicant an opportunity to make representations in reply.

9 *Fairmount Investments Ltd v Secretary of State for the Environment* [1976] 1 WLR 1255, HL at 1266.

10 At the time of finalising the book (July 2024), the established position is that the standards of consultation are the same whether the consultation was conducted in compliance with a duty or on a 'voluntary' basis. However, it is anticipated that a defendant to a 'voluntary' consultation claim may seek to argue that the standards of fairness do not apply in such cases, and that the governing principle is irrationality. This issue was raised but not determined by the Court of Appeal in *R (Secretary of State for Work and Pensions) v Eveleigh* [2023] EWCA Civ 810 ('*Eveleigh*').

principle to note at the outset is that the standard of fairness in consultation is the same, whether a decision-maker chooses to consult voluntarily or is under a duty to do so.[11] However, whether a decision-maker has chosen to 'consult' as a matter of law, rather than merely gathering information, depends on all the circumstances of the case, including whether there is a specific proposal which is at the appropriate stage for consultation.[12]

2.11 Following the Court of Appeal's judgment in *Eveleigh*, it is now clear that a public body can gather information, can describe what it is doing as 'consulting', but still not be 'consulting' as a matter of law, in a way which triggers the obligations of common law fairness. The question is one of substance not form – as above, focusing on whether there is a specific proposal which is at the appropriate stage for consultation.

2.12 Before making a decision, it is important that the decision-maker gives consideration to whether the law obliges them to consult with affected parties, whether individuals, groups and/or the public at large. Indeed, regardless of whether consultation is actually required by law, the decision-maker may in any event wish to undertake a consultation to help them make a decision that is well informed and to show that the views of others have been taken into account. As such, it is relatively rare now that the issue is *whether* a decision-maker has to consult.[13] Rather, the dispute is more likely to be over what fair consultation requires in the particular circumstances.

Decisions affecting particular individuals

2.13 Where a decision directly affects an individual, the decision-maker will have to:

(1) inform the individual that a decision is going to be taken;
(2) provide the individual with sufficient information to allow them to participate effectively in the decision-making process;
(3) allow the individual to make representations;

11 *R v North and East Devon HA ex p Coughlan* [2001] QB 213, CA at [108]. However, see footnote 10 above as to the argument on this in *Eveleigh*.

12 *Eveleigh*, footnote 10 above.

13 For an example of such a case, see *Binder and others v Secretary of State for Work and Pensions* [2022] EWHC 105 (Admin) at first instance (which became *Eveleigh* on appeal), where the issue was whether the secretary of state had voluntarily consulted on the National Disability Strategy, and, if not, whether he was under a common law duty to have done so.

(4) give them adequate time to do so; and
(5) take any representations made into account before making the decision.

2.14 Depending on the context, what fairness requires may be set out in statute or in guidance. For example, there is detailed guidance from the Department for Education on the process for making decisions about suspending and permanently excluding children from school that schools and local authorities are expected to follow.[14]

2.15 In these cases, it is vital that the process adopted is accessible to the individual and takes account of their needs. For example, guidance from the Department of Health and Social Care[15] sets out in some detail the approach to be followed by NHS bodies when making eligibility decisions for NHS-funded care (known as 'continuing healthcare' or 'CHC'). That guidance requires a 'person-centred' approach which includes:

(1) ensuring that the individual and/or their representative is fully and directly involved in the assessment process;
(2) taking full account of the individual's own views and wishes, ensuring that their perspective is incorporated in the assessment process;
(3) addressing communication and language needs;
(4) obtaining consent to any physical intervention/examination as part of the assessment process (where the individual has capacity to give this);
(5) obtaining consent to the sharing of personal data with third parties (eg family, friends, advocates and/or other representatives) (where the individual has capacity to give this);
(6) dealing openly with issues of risk; and
(7) keeping the individual (and/or their representative) fully informed.[16]

2.16 Most of these principles are transferrable to other contexts where an important decision is being made about an individual.

14 Department for Education *Suspension and permanent exclusion from maintained schools, academies and pupil referral units in England, including pupil movement* (September 2023).

15 *National framework for NHS continuing healthcare and NHS-funded nursing care* (July 2023).

16 *National framework for NHS continuing healthcare and NHS-funded nursing care* para 69.

Decisions affecting groups or the public at large

When does the duty to consult arise?

2.17 Where a public body makes a decision that affects a group of people or the public at large, it may be required to consult before making the decision.

2.18 The courts have repeatedly stressed that there is no general obligation to consult. The obligation to consult only arises where there is a duty to do so under legislation or at common law. These circumstances can be categorised as follows:[17]

(1) *There is a statutory duty to consult.* Where the duty to consult is imposed by legislation, it is important to consider carefully the exact wording of the relevant statutory provision, because it may specify in some detail the circumstances in which consultation is required and what the consultation must cover, including any specified individuals and/or groups who must be consulted.

(2) *A legitimate expectation has arisen that consultation will take place.* This generally requires a clear and unequivocal promise from the relevant public body that it will consult. Alternatively, if the public body has an established practice of consulting on the same or similar cases then this may also give rise to a legitimate expectation that consultation will take place. See further chapter 4 at para 4.83.

(3) *It would be conspicuously unfair for the body not to consult.* This category of cases will be exceptional cases, given that the common law usually requires there to be a legitimate expectation based on a promise or past practice for the duty to consult to arise.[18]

2.19 An obligation to consult may also arise as a result of the public sector equality duty (PSED) (the obligation in Equality Act 2010 s149 that public bodies have 'due regard' to equalities impacts in the exercise of their functions). This is because the courts have held that the PSED incorporates a duty of inquiry such that, if a public body lacks the information it needs to understand the equalities impacts of a decision, it is obliged to acquire the information in question.[19]

17 *R (Plantagenet Alliance Ltd) v Secretary of State for Justice* [2014] EWHC 1662 (Admin) at [98](2).

18 An example of a 'conspicuous unfairness' case is *R (Luton BC) v Secretary of State for Education* [2011] EWHC 556 (Admin), where the secretary of state abruptly halted the Building Schools for the Future programme without prior consultation.

19 *R (Hurley and Moore) v Secretary of State for Business, Innovation and Skills* [2012] EWHC 201 (Admin) at [89]–[90].

In some circumstances, the only way of obtaining the information is through consultation, and so this is what is required. Nonetheless, it is important to recognise that public bodies have considerable discretion in this regard – for the need to obtain further information to be a legal obligation it must be shown that it was irrational not to do so.[20] The PSED is discussed further in chapter 5 at para 5.85 onwards.

What does the duty to consult require?

2.20 Where a public body is subject to a duty to consult (or chooses to consult even though it does not have to[21]), the consultation undertaken must be fair. There are four main requirements[22] for a consultation to be fair:

(1) consultation is undertaken at a time when the relevant proposal is still at a formative stage;
(2) adequate information is provided to consultees to enable them properly to respond to the consultation exercise;
(3) consultees are afforded adequate time in which to respond; and
(4) the decision-maker gives conscientious consideration to consultees' responses.

2.21 In respect of (2), there is ongoing debate as to the extent to which public bodies are required to consult on options other than their main proposal. It is lawful for a public body to indicate in a consultation document what its preferred option is,[23] and there is no general obligation to consult on proposals that a public body is not proposing.[24] Nonetheless, a consultation will be unlawful if the information provided gives the misleading impression that there are no viable options other than those being consulted on.[25] Furthermore, sometimes public bodies will be required to consult on arguable yet discarded alternative options as a matter of fairness.[26]

2.22 In respect of (3), what constitutes 'adequate time' for consultation will depend on all the circumstances. However, in the authors' experience, any consultation which is at least six weeks long is likely to be

20 *R (Hollow) v Surrey CC* [2019] EWHC 618 (Admin) at [84].
21 See footnote 10 above for the controversy on this point in the Court of Appeal in *Eveleigh*.
22 Commonly known as the *Gunning* requirements, from *R v Brent LBC ex p Gunning* (1985) 84 LGR 168, QBD.
23 *R (Moseley) v Haringey LBC* [2014] UKSC 56 at [27]–[28].
24 *Bailey and others v Brent LBC* [2011] EWHC 2572 (Admin) at [90].
25 *Moseley* at [29].
26 *Moseley* at [27].

treated as 'adequate', unless there are exceptional circumstances pointing in the other direction.

2.23 Finally, in respect of (4) it is important to remember that ultimately consultation is a procedural rather than a substantive obligation. That means that while decision-makers have to take into account the consultation responses received, they are not obliged to make any particular decision as a result of the consultation responses. However, if the vast majority of consultees prefer option A in a consultation, and the decision-maker decides instead to choose option B, it is likely that fairness will require the decision-maker to acknowledge this and provide at least some explanation as to the reasons for their choice.

Bias

2.24 Decisions must not be made that either are biased or *appear* to be biased. In other words, decisions should not be, nor appear to be, influenced by preconceived prejudices or inclinations (whether conscious or unconscious). This is because decisions must not just be fair, but be *seen to be* fair.

2.25 The legal test developed by the courts is: whether the fair-minded and informed observer, having considered the factual background of the decision, would conclude that there was a real possibility that the decision-maker was biased. The fair-minded and informed observer is not unduly sensitive or suspicious, but neither are they complacent.[27]

Appearance of bias

2.26 Personal or professional relationships with the subjects of the decision can give rise to a risk of the decision-maker appearing biased. Equally, a personal or professional interest in the outcome of a decision will also give risk to the risk of a biased decision. As an obvious example, if a member of a planning committee lives next door to the site of the proposed planning application, then that person should not take part in the decision so as to avoid a risk of appearance of bias (even if that person has no personal view on the application).

27 *Gillies v Secretary of State for Work and Pensions* [2006] UKHL 2 at [17] per Lord Hope and [39] per Baroness Hale.

2.27 If the decision-maker takes part in a determination or appeal against one of their own decisions, or one in which they had participated, then they risk an appearance of bias arising.[28]

2.28 Decision-makers must be transparent in relation to communications with parties, otherwise there is the risk of an appearance of bias. Decision-makers should not communicate with just one party. Where there is unavoidable unilateral communication, such as if a decision-maker receives an unexpected phone call from one of the parties, then the other party should be informed as soon as possible. The decision-maker should keep a careful record of any such communications and make sure that the relevant party knows that what is said or written will need to be communicated to the other parties.

Practical approach to making unbiased decisions

2.29 If a court finds that a decision was biased, or appeared to be biased, it will overturn that decision. It is therefore important to identify and address any risks of appearing to be biased before making a decision.

2.30 To ensure transparency, any interests in the decision-making process (no matter how minor they seem) should be declared to the parties, who should be given a proper opportunity to object on that basis. Moreover, any participants in a decision-making process who could realistically appear to be biased should 'recuse' themselves (ie withdraw from the decision-making and take no further part in it). It is important to emphasise that a decision-maker does not need actually to be biased for a decision to be flawed in law. Indeed, in almost all circumstances of appearance of bias, the decision-maker is not actually biased (or at least there is insufficient evidence to make such a finding, on the balance of probabilities).

2.31 A court's assessment of whether or not a decision was biased (actual or apparent) will be sensitive to the particular facts. However, where in doubt, it is better to pass the decision on to someone else to make rather than risk the decision being vulnerable to challenge. It would only be in a rare situation where there is no other effective way of making the decision that it may be appropriate for a decision-maker who risks appearing to be biased (but in fact is not) to proceed to take the decision.

28 For example, a lay representative who served on a disciplinary panel conducting a hearing into a disciplinary matter concerning a barrister was held to be disqualified by reason of the fact that she had attended a meeting of the Professional Conduct Committee which had decided to prosecute the barrister: *P (a barrister) v General Council of the Bar* [2005] 1 WLR 3019, Visitors to the Inns of Court.

Conflicts of interest

2.32 A conflict of interest arises where there is a risk that a decision-maker's ability to execute their role or exercise judgment may be influenced by a secondary interest. That conflict of interest may be actual or potential. There is a close link between these principles and those in relation to actual or apparent bias, discussed above.

2.33 The aim of assessing conflicts of interest is not to eliminate conflicts entirely, since that may be impossible in areas of specialist expertise. Conflicts of interest are often context specific and will need to be assessed on a case-by-case basis. Therefore, the approach is one of principles, rather than set rules.

2.34 There are some general principles that it will be helpful to bear in mind in assessing a potential conflict of interest:

(1) There are several markers that might indicate a potential conflict of interest. These include personal relationships, pecuniary interests such as where a decision-maker has a direct or indirect financial interest in a particular outcome, concurrent work (whether paid or unpaid), previous employment, political interests, and accepting gifts or hospitality.
(2) Consider whether there is legislation which specifies that the relevant decision-maker must publish guidance on the discharge of their functions regarding conflicts of interests and have regard to that guidance.
(3) Decision-makers should know how to identify and report actual or potential conflicts of interest.
(4) Decision-makers should routinely declare any potential interests and keep potential conflicts of interest under review.
(5) Where a conflict of interest nonetheless arises, the decision-maker should consider whether it is appropriate to inform the parties to the decision, whether it is possible and appropriate to abandon the interest and/or whether it is appropriate for the decision-maker to continue being involved in the matter.
(6) If there is a risk of a conflict of interest, the decision-maker should seek to transfer the matter to an alternative decision-maker.

Notice

2.35 It is an important part of the decision-making process that any person impacted by a decision knows in advance that a decision is being made and knows how to participate in the process. The requirement of notice of a decision is consequently closely related to the right to be consulted or heard (discussed earlier in this chapter).

2.36 Without prior notice of a decision, it will be difficult to conclude that a person has had an adequate opportunity to make representations. As such, notice must be served with sufficient time to allow representations to be made effectively.

Notice requirements

2.37 The principles of natural justice and procedural fairness generally require that those impacted by a decision are entitled to know the case that they have to meet and be given a reasonable opportunity to put forward evidence and make submissions in response.

2.38 Procedural fairness therefore requires that those who may be affected by a decision or administrative act are given adequate notice of the proposed decision so that they can respond to that decision.[29] It should not be the case that those affected are 'surprised' by the decision.[30] There are cases where no notice whatsoever was given and this failure to give notice effectively amounted to a denial of an opportunity to be heard.[31]

2.39 However, as awareness of the basic requirements of procedural fairness has increased, the number of cases that concern a total lack of notice being given has decreased. Focus has now shifted to challenges regarding the extent of the notice given and whether this has been adequate.

29 See eg *Re JR17's Application for Judicial Review (Northern Ireland)* [2010] UKSC 27 at [50]: 'a person's right to have afforded to him a reasonable opportunity of learning what is alleged against him and of putting forward his own case in answer to it is "one of the fundamental rights accorded by the common law rules of natural justice" '.

30 In *R (Anufrijeva) v Secretary of State for the Home Department* [2003] UKHL 36 at [30] Lord Steyn stated that '[i]n our system of law surprise is regarded as the enemy of justice'.

31 In *R (Shoesmith) v Ofsted* [2011] EWCA Civ 642, although there had been urgency, it had not been such as to necessitate such a truncation of the requirements of fairness as occurred in that case. See further, *R (L) v Commissioner of Police of the Metropolis* [2009] UKSC 3, in the context of disclosure of information in an enhanced criminal record certificate without notice to the applicant, the Supreme Court holding she should have been afforded an opportunity to make representations prior to the certificate being issued.

2.40 The following principles are helpful to bear in mind:

(1) Relevant statutory rules may set out the requirements for giving notice in particular circumstances. Decision-makers should check to see if any relevant rules apply.
(2) Fairness will very often require that a person who may be adversely affected by the decision will have an opportunity to make representations, most commonly before the decision is taken. Since the person affected usually cannot make worthwhile representations without knowing what factors may weigh against their interests, fairness will very often require that the person is informed of the substance of the case which they have to answer.[32]
(3) In individual cases, unless a statute expressly or impliedly excludes it, or in the particular case it would be impractical or frustrate the object of the direction, fairness may well require that a person specifically targeted by a decision should have an opportunity to make representations.[33] Therefore, those affected by a decision must receive notice of a decision and have the opportunity to make representations before the decision is made.[34]
(4) It may be the case that a large number of people might be impacted by a particular decision. In those circumstances, public notice must be in such terms as are fairly and reasonably necessary to enable members of the public in the area affected to learn of the decisions and to make objections where they wish to do so.[35]
(5) In circumstances where a decision is likely to impact a particular individual and cause them loss, the duty is higher and the individual must be notified.[36]
(6) Except in special circumstances such as an emergency, any person who will be impacted by a decision must be given a fair opportunity to make any relevant statement and therefore notice is important.[37]

32 *R v Secretary of State for the Home Department ex p Doody* [1994] 1 AC 531, HL at 560.

33 *Bank Mellat v HM Treasury* [2013] UKSC 39 at [32].

34 *Bank Mellat v HM Treasury* [2013] UKSC 39 at [28].

35 *Wilson v Secretary of State for the Environment* [1973] 1 WLR 1083, QBD.

36 *R v Ealing Justices ex p Fanneran* (1996) 160 JP 409, QBD concerned a judicial review of the decision to make a destruction order in relation to a pit bull terrier. The complaint was that the owner of the pit bull terrier had not been informed of the hearing. The handler of the dog at the time, her nephew, had been informed. The court allowed the application and held that whilst the owner's presence at the hearing may not have made any difference to the outcome, a breach of natural justice had occurred as the owner should have been informed of the hearing.

37 *De Verteuil v Knaggs and another* [1918] AC 557, PC (Trinidad and Tobago) at 560.

(7) However, in some circumstances the decision-maker will not be at fault where notice does not reach the individual affected. For example, where notice is not given because of an error made by the individual's solicitor.[38] In those circumstances, the decision-maker has done all that they reasonably can. Further, the individual might already have known or have been aware and so notice was unnecessary.[39]

(8) Where there is inadequate notice this is capable of invalidating subsequent legal proceedings.[40] However, there are exceptions to this general rule in statute. The question then is one of whether prejudice has been caused, such that failing to give notice is a ground for setting aside the decision.[41]

Data protection

2.41 The protection of personal data is regulated by the EU General Data Protection Regulation[42] (GDPR) and the Data Protection Act (DPA) 2018. The EU GDPR has been transposed into domestic law following Brexit. The legislative regime applies to public bodies and private companies alike, but it also includes specific rules that apply only to public bodies. It is important to ensure compliance with the regime, as breaches of the rules may result in significant financial penalties. Infringements of the basic principles for processing personal data are subject to the highest tier of administrative fines, which could

38 In *R (Nori) v Secretary of State for the Home Department* [2011] EWHC 1604 (Admin) the court said at [48] that 'as a general proposition the failure of a solicitor is to be equated with a failure of the individual'.

39 *Byrne v Kinematograph Renters Society* [1958] 1 WLR 762, ChD at 785.

40 See eg *R (London Reading College Ltd) v Secretary of State for the Home Department* [2010] EWHC 2561 (Admin) where at [54] the court held that '[t]he making of a decision without giving the chance to address the principle matters of complaint is a breach of the requirements of procedural fairness and it must lead to the quashing of the decision'.

41 See eg Town and Country Planning Act 1990 s176(5), which provides that:

> Where it would otherwise be a ground for determining an appeal under section 174 in favour of the appellant that a person required to be served with a copy of the enforcement notice was not served, the Secretary of State may disregard that fact if neither the appellant nor that person has been substantially prejudiced by the failure to serve him.

42 Regulation (EU) 2016/679 of the European Parliament and of the Council of 27 April 2016 on the protection of natural persons with regard to the processing of personal data and on the free movement of such data, and repealing Directive 95/46/EC.

result in a fine of up to £17.5 million. This section briefly highlights some of the key provisions that may be relevant to decision-makers. Further detail is available from the Information Commissioner's Office (ICO).[43]

2.42 Every person responsible for using personal data has to comply with the 'data protection principles', which are explained below. If a person is responsible for dealing with special categories of personal data, even stricter rules apply. These rules will apply to decision-makers as to any other person.

What is personal data and special category personal data?

2.43 Personal data is information relating to natural persons who:

- can be identified or who are identifiable, directly from the information in question; or
- can be indirectly identified from that information in combination with other information.

2.44 Special category personal data is particularly sensitive, and consists of data relating to racial or ethnic origin, political opinions, religious or philosophical beliefs, trade union membership, genetic data, biometric data, data concerning health, or data concerning a natural person's sex life or sexual orientation. As such, it is important not to be misled by the term 'special category' – these categories of data can include data commonly held by a range of bodies. For example, a person's medical records will constitute special category data.

Who is responsible? Data controllers and processors

2.45 Different obligations apply to users of personal data, depending on whether they are classified as data controllers or processors:

- *Controllers*: Controllers exercise overall control over the purposes and means of the processing of personal data. For example, controllers will have decided to collect or process the personal data, and what the purpose or outcome of the processing should be.
- *Processors*: Processors act on behalf of, and only on the instructions of, the relevant controller. Processors will not decide, for example, what personal data should be collected from individuals, and for what purpose.

43 https://ico.org.uk/

2.46 Controllers have the highest level of responsibility, and must be able to demonstrate compliance with all the data protection principles as well as the other GDPR requirements. By contrast, processors do not have the same obligations, but nonetheless must comply with certain requirements. Controllers are responsible for the compliance of their processors. Supervisory authorities (such as the ICO), as well as individuals, may take action against both controllers and processors in the event of a breach of their data protection requirements.

The data protection principles

2.47 The data protection principles contained in the GDPR are as follows.

Lawfulness, fairness and transparency

2.48 In order to ensure your data use is lawful, you must identify valid grounds under the GDPR (a 'lawful basis') for collecting and using personal data. There are six lawful bases, which include, for example, consent, contract, legal obligation, 'vital interests' and conducting a public task. This demonstrates that consent is not always necessary in data processing, and may often not be the most appropriate lawful basis. In order to rely upon the lawful basis of 'public task', the processing must be necessary for you to perform a task in the public interest or for your official functions, and the task or function must have a clear basis in law.

2.49 For special category personal data, a further, more onerous, processing condition must be satisfied. For example, the individual must have given 'explicit' consent, or the processing must be necessary to protect the vital interests of the data subject. Moreover, you must also ensure that you do not do anything with the data in breach of any other laws, such as infringing copyright or breaching a duty of confidence.

2.50 You must use personal data in a way that is fair. This means you must not process the data in a way that is misleading, unexpected or excessively detrimental to the individuals concerned.

2.51 In order to ensure transparency, you must be clear, open and honest with people from the start about how you will use their personal data. It is necessary to explain your purposes for processing their personal data, your retention periods for that personal data, and who it will be shared with, using plain language, so that your explanation is easily accessible and easy to understand. You must bring any new uses of an individual's personal data to their attention before you start the processing.

Purpose limitation

2.52 The purpose limitation principle requires that you must be clear about what your purposes are before you start processing data. These purposes need to be documented, and specified in the privacy information provided for individuals as part of your transparency obligations. You may only use the personal data for a new purpose if either this is compatible with your original purpose, you get consent or you have a clear basis in law. If you originally collected the data on the basis of consent, you would usually need to seek the individuals' fresh consent to ensure your new processing is fair and lawful.

Data minimisation

2.53 In order to comply with this principle, personal data you are processing must be:

(1) adequate;
(2) relevant; and
(3) limited to what is necessary. You should periodically review the data you hold, and delete anything you no longer need.

Accuracy

2.54 Reasonable steps should be taken to ensure the personal data you hold is not incorrect or misleading as to any matter of fact. If any challenges are made to the accuracy of personal data, they must be carefully considered and remedial steps taken where appropriate (see the right to rectification at para 2.62 below).

Storage limitation

2.55 Data must not be kept for longer than necessary.

Integrity and confidentiality (security)

2.56 Appropriate security measures must be in place. These would involve, for example, adequate firewalls, encryption and physical storage of hard copies of personal data.

Accountability

2.57 It is necessary to ensure that compliance with the data protection principles can be demonstrated. Therefore, it is important to be proactive and organised in keeping full records of data processing.

Adopting and maintaining data protection policies, and making them available on your website, also helps to make sure your accountability measures are transparent.

Further practical steps required for compliance

2.58 Further practical steps which are required for compliance with the regime, include training staff, conducting data protection impact assessments and notifying the ICO within 72 hours if you breach the regulations.

Individual rights

2.59 The GDPR provides individuals with a number of rights, which can be exercised in writing or verbally. Requests should be appropriately recorded. You must respond to a request from a person seeking to exercise one of their rights below within one month. Some of the rights of particular relevance to decision-makers are as follows.

The right to be informed

2.60 Individuals have the right to be provided with clear and concise information about how, and why, their personal data is processed.

The right of access

2.61 An individual is entitled to confirmation that you are processing their personal data, and a copy of their personal data. It is important that no information is provided that relates to others. You also must provide certain additional information, such as the purposes for which their data was processed; the existence of their right to request rectification, erasure or restriction or to object to such processing; and the right to lodge a complaint with the ICO or another supervisory authority.

The right to rectification

2.62 Individuals also have a right to have inaccurate personal data rectified, or completed if it is incomplete. You should take reasonable steps to satisfy yourself that the data is accurate and then rectify the data if necessary. If you are satisfied the data is in fact accurate, then inform the individual that you will not be amending the data, explain why and inform them of their right to make a complaint to the ICO.

The right to restrict processing

2.63 Individuals have the right to request you restrict the processing of their personal data. Restricting the processing of personal data may involve, for example, making the data unavailable to users, or temporarily removing published data from a website. An individual may exercise their right in the following circumstances:

(1) the individual contests the accuracy of their personal data and you are checking the accuracy of the data;
(2) the data has been unlawfully processed, and the individual opposes deletion and requests restriction instead;
(3) you no longer need the personal data but the individual needs you to keep it in order to establish, exercise or defend a legal claim; or
(4) the individual has objected to you on the basis that you do not have legitimate grounds for processing their data.

Confidentiality

2.64 Decision-makers may also owe duties of confidentiality in relation to certain information. If a person provides personal or sensitive information to you in circumstances where they have a reasonable expectation of confidence, then you must not use or disclose that information without their consent. Disclosure may only be justified without that person's consent where there is a legal requirement to do so, or, in some cases, where the interests of the individual, third parties or the general public demands it. Any decision to disclose confidential information in such circumstances must be carefully documented.

2.65 There is a particularly strong steer in the government guidance in relation to children that concerns as to confidentiality or data protection should not prevent information being shared that may help keep children safe.[44]

44 See Department for Education *Information sharing: advice for practitioners providing safeguarding services for children, young people, parents and carers* (May 2024).

Disclosure

2.66 It is a fundamental rule of procedural fairness that as part of any kind of regulatory or disciplinary process a person is told of allegations made against them, and must be given a fair opportunity of responding to them.[45] The allegations must be explained in a sufficiently detailed form so that the person can make meaningful objections or put forward meaningful representations.[46] This applies equally to adverse points made against the subject of a decision more broadly. In order to satisfy this obligation, it will usually be necessary to provide the person concerned with relevant evidence or information.[47]

2.67 The disclosure process can often be administratively inconvenient. However, it is a necessary and important limb of procedural fairness.

2.68 Providing full and proper disclosure will also help to ensure that the obligation to provide sufficient reasons is also met (see chapter 4 at para 4.107 onwards), as the provision of the documents underlying a decision will help to ensure the subject of that decision can understand it.

2.69 If the relevant material has not been disclosed to the person subject to the decision, and they are prejudiced as a result, then the decision will be unfair, and at serious risk of a successful challenge.

What must be disclosed?

2.70 At a minimum, the decision-maker should disclose the evidence or information that is relevant to the decision, and influential material on which the decision-maker intends to rely.[48] For example, if a decision is made to hold a disciplinary hearing in relation to an individual, the decision-maker must provide the person with the evidence and information relied upon. This may include an investigatory

45 *Council of Civil Service Unions v Minister for the Civil Service* [1985] AC 374, HL at 415; *Hadmor Productions v Hamilton* [1983] 1 AC 191, HL at 233 per Lord Diplock.

46 *R (Benson) v Secretary of State for Justice* [2007] EWHC 2055 (Admin) at [22].

47 See eg *R (Ramda) v Secretary of State for the Home Department* [2002] EWHC 1278 (Admin) at [25]; *R (Banks) v Secretary of State for the Environment, Food and Rural Affairs* [2004] EWHC 416 (Admin) at [104].

48 See eg *R (O'Leary) v Chief Constable of Merseyside* [2001] EWHC Admin 57 at [16].

report, or documents such as emails or photographs, which underpin the allegations made against them.

2.71 In addition to providing evidence that is detrimental to the individual, it is also necessary to disclose material that is favourable to them if relevant to the decision. This also helps to ensure that the decision is adequately reasoned, as the points favourable to the individual, as well as those against them, should be addressed.

2.72 Representations or information provided by third parties may also be required to be disclosed. For example, letters of complaint or objections submitted to the decision-maker by third parties which have been relied upon should be provided to the subject of the decision, so that they have a fair opportunity to respond to their contents.[49]

2.73 In assessing whether documents should be disclosed in respect of a particular decision, the purpose of the disclosure must be borne in mind. The person must not be prevented from correcting or commenting on the evidence or information relied upon in respect of the decision.[50]

2.74 Moreover, it should also be remembered that if the decision is challenged by way of an application for judicial review, a special duty of disclosure would apply anyway which would require the parties to ensure that all relevant information and all material facts are put before the court. This would include all material which may either support or undermine their case. This duty is known as the 'duty of candour'.[51] However, compliance with the duty of candour does not necessarily require disclosure of actual documents, if the relevant

49 See: *R (Anglian Water Services Ltd) v Environment Agency* [2003] EWHC 1506 (Admin), in which Owen J held that the Environment Agency's failure to provide letters from residents relied upon in making an adverse decision against the water company was a breach of procedural fairness.

50 *R (O'Leary) v Chief Constable of Merseyside* [2001] EWHC Admin 57 at [16].

51 *R (Al-Sweady and others) v Secretary of State for Defence* [2009] EWHC 2387 (Admin) at [22]:

> This obligation is a very important one because of the special position of the public authority and indeed it has been said that there is 'a very high duty on public authority respondents, not least central government, to assist the court with full and accurate explanation of all the facts relevant to the issue the court must decide' (per Laws LJ in *R (Quark Fishing Limited) v Secretary of State for Foreign and Commonwealth Affairs* [2002] EWCA Civ 1409 [50]).

See also: *R v Secretary of State for the Home Department ex p Al-Fayed (No 1)* [1998] 1 WLR 763, CA at 775 per Lord Woolf MR: 'On an application for judicial review there is usually no [disclosure] because [disclosure] should be unnecessary because it is the obligation of the [defendant] public body in its evidence to make frank disclosure to the court of the decision-making process.'

information can be provided in a different form (for example, in a witness statement).[52]

At what stage of the process should disclosure be made?

2.75 Usually, it is best to provide the evidence and information as early in the process as practicable. This helps to ensure that the concerned individual or individuals has an adequate opportunity to make representations in respect of that documentation.

2.76 In decisions involving oral hearings, if evidence or information is not able to be provided until the hearing itself, fairness will usually require that the hearing is adjourned so that the person concerned has a proper opportunity to respond.[53] In order to avoid such delays (and the risk of criticism by the tribunal), disclosure should be made well in advance of a hearing.

When is disclosure not required?

2.77 There are limited circumstances in which disclosure is not required, in particular the following.

Risk to public interest

2.78 If disclosure would cause harm to the public interest, because it would, for example, involve sharing official secrets or inhibit the detection of crime.[54]

Privilege

2.79 Legal advice, or documents created for the purpose of (existing or contemplated) litigation, may be withheld on the basis that they are legally privileged.[55]

52 See *R (Police Superintendents' Association) v Police Remuneration Review Body* [2023] EWHC 1838 (Admin) for detailed guidance on when the duty of candour requires documents to be provided.

53 *R (Agogo) v North Somerset Magistrates' Court* [2011] EWHC 518 (Admin) at [15].

54 *R v Lewes Justices ex p Gaming Board for Great Britain* [1973] AC 388, HL; *R v Secretary of State for the Home Department ex p Hickey* [1995] QB 43, CA; *R v Chief Constable of the West Midlands ex p Wiley* [1995] 1 AC 274, HL.

55 See eg *Director of the Serious Fraud Office v Eurasian Natural Resources Corp Ltd* [2017] EWHC 1017 (QB).

Confidentiality

2.80 The disclosure would be a breach of confidence owed to a third party.[56]

2.81 Whether a particular document is subject to a proper claim of public interest immunity, confidentiality or privilege should be determined with the help of specialist legal advice on a case-by-case basis. It is important to bear in mind that a document may only be partly exempt from the obligation to be disclosed, and the confidential or privileged parts of a document could be addressed through appropriate redactions, for example.

56 *R v Poole BC ex p Cooper* (1995) 27 HLR 605, QBD; *R v Joint Higher Committee on Surgical Training ex p Milner* (1995) 7 Admin LR 454, QBD.

CHAPTER 3

Hearings

continued

Holding an oral hearing

3.1 Where an oral hearing is required or deemed appropriate, there are a number of questions about the form a hearing should take. The purposes of a hearing are generally to ensure that:

- those concerned with the decision can present evidence and make representations; and
- those making the decision can obtain all the relevant information and, where appropriate, test the evidence presented to them.

Providing information in advance

3.2 It is important to remember that many people will not have experience of 'hearings' or similar formal situations and may not know what to expect if they are told a hearing is to take place. As such, clear information should be provided to the relevant people in advance as to who will be present, what their roles will be, the procedure that will be followed (see table at para 3.8 below) and anything an individual might be expected to bring (for example, if they should bring documentary evidence with them or submit documents in advance). Parties should also be told whether they are allowed to bring a representative, and whether that person can be a lawyer.

3.3 It is also a good idea (and may be necessary to avoid discrimination) to provide clear information about the location of the venue, how to get there and what facilities will be available. Inquiry should be made in advance as to whether any person who will be participating in the hearing has a disability or any other needs that may affect the choice of venue, or require adaptations to the venue and/or the format of the hearing, in order to ensure compliance with duties under the Equality Act 2010 (see chapter 5).[1]

3.4 It is important to ensure that a person participating in the hearing is given enough notice of the date and scope of the hearing to enable them properly to prepare, without unduly delaying the decision-making process (see further chapter 2 at para 2.35 onwards re notice). If a person is not given adequate notice so that they can properly prepare for the hearing, there is a risk that a court might conclude they have not been given a fair hearing at all.

1 For general guidance on non-discrimination issues, see Equality and Human Rights Commission *Services, public functions and associations: Code of Practice* (January 2011).

Form and procedure

3.5 Hearings can take many different forms. Sometimes the relevant legislation or case-law will spell out aspects of how a hearing should be conducted. Sometimes guidance will have been issued by a relevant body as to how the hearing should be conducted. It is essential to ensure that any statutory requirements are met, and that any applicable guidance is considered (or followed, depending on its specific legal status). This chapter is intended to provide guidance on the general factors to consider, particularly where neither statute nor published guidance provides a specific answer.

3.6 Where an oral hearing is to be held, it is for the decision-maker to determine the form that the hearing should take, provided that the form of the hearing is fair to everyone taking part and those who may be affected by the decision.

3.7 What fairness requires in a particular context will depend on a wide range of factors including:

- the nature of the decision;
- whether there is likely to be any dispute about the relevant facts and, if so, what sort of evidence will help to resolve the dispute;
- who the decision will affect;
- the importance of the decision to those affected;
- the steps needed to enable those affected to participate effectively;
- the need to enable equality of arms between the participants;
- the resources available to the decision-maker; and
- the need to ensure that decision-making is not unduly prolonged.

3.8 The decision-maker should give careful consideration to the procedure that will be followed at the hearing, and explain this clearly to the relevant people in advance. Matters to be considered include the following:

Before the hearing	• Whether the people taking part are permitted or required to submit evidence and/or written representations before the hearing and, if so, the format and deadline for doing so and whether this has been explained to those taking part • Whether the people taking part have had access to all the evidence, including the 'bundle' or papers provided to the decision-maker

At the hearing	• The time the hearing will begin • The scheduled order of events at the hearing • How long the hearing is expected to last • Whether the hearing will be in public or private • Whether the people taking part are permitted to bring people along with them to the hearing to help them and/or to speak on their behalf • Who will be permitted to speak, when and for how long • Who will be permitted to ask questions, and of whom • What evidence will be available at the hearing to the decision-maker to consider when reaching their decision • How the people taking part will be able to refer to documents and evidence at the hearing
After the hearing	• Whether the decision-maker will make a decision on the same day as the hearing or, if not, when • How the decision-maker will give the people affected their decision and the reasons for that decision • How and when the people affected will be informed of any appeal process or other potential route of challenge (for example, judicial review)

In public or private?

3.9 Where an oral hearing is to be held, which may be required in relation to more important decisions, it is generally in the interests of transparent decision-making that any hearing should be in public. This reflects the important principle of open justice. But there may be reasons why a public hearing is not appropriate, or indeed may be unlawful. You will need to consider factors including:

- the nature of the decision;
- the sort of information that will be presented, in particular whether it may involve confidential or sensitive personal information;
- whether there is a wider public interest in the process or outcome of the decision;
- what the effect of holding a hearing in public is likely to be on those involved; and
- any particular vulnerability of those involved, in particular if anyone is a child.

3.10 For example, where a hearing is to be held in relation to a proposal to close a public facility that plays an important role in the lives of those who use it, a public hearing is likely to be appropriate. By contrast, where a hearing is to be held to determine a matter affecting one particular individual, where sensitive personal information will be at the heart of the decision to be taken, it may be more appropriate for the hearing to be held in private.

3.11 Whether a hearing should be in public or private is not necessarily a binary choice. For example, where it is desirable that a hearing should be in public, but there is particular evidence that needs to be kept confidential, it may be possible to hold part of the hearing in private and/or to accept and consider the confidential material in anonymised form or provide a 'gist' of that material to the public so that they can make representations.

3.12 Special considerations apply where the hearing concerns children. Decisions as to the form of a hearing should have regard to the best interests of the child as a primary consideration.[2] In practice, it will generally be appropriate for hearings affecting individual children to be held in private (as happens in most judicial proceedings concerned with education, for example). On the other hand, if a hearing were held in relation to the closure of a facility used by children and a child wished to express their views in a public forum, it may be in their best interests to enable them to do so. It is important to keep in mind that a child under 16 may be competent to express their own views, and a 16- or 17-year-old child benefits from the presumption of mental capacity in the Mental Capacity Act 2005.[3]

3.13 Special considerations will also apply where the hearing concerns a person who lacks capacity to participate in a hearing or to make their own decisions about the matters under consideration (including whether there should be publicity) because of a mental disability or disorder. There may be stronger arguments for a hearing to take place in private in these circumstances.

Legal adviser

3.14 Some decision-makers operate under a statutory framework that permits or requires a legal adviser to be present at a hearing. Legal advisers are not decision-makers themselves. Their role is to provide legal advice to the decision-makers, and generally they are required to provide that advice transparently and in the presence of the people

2 Reflecting the overarching obligation in Article 3 of the UN Convention on the Rights of the Child.

3 Guidance on the law governing decision making by children and young people can found in S Broach KC and L Clements *Disabled Children: a legal handbook* (Legal Action Group, 3rd ed, 2020), chapter 7.

participating in the hearing, so that any disagreement with the legal advice can be aired.

Evidence, witnesses and questioning

3.15 A hearing is not a trial and the rules of evidence and procedures of a civil or criminal court are not necessarily an appropriate model for other hearings. It is better to ask in any particular situation what procedure in relation to evidence and witnesses will enable a fully informed decision, including allowing those affected to provide relevant information and representations. The procedure adopted should be proportionate to the issues at stake.

The importance of sufficient notice to enable appropriate preparation

3.16 It is important to make clear to those participating in a hearing what evidence, if any, will be expected in advance of the hearing, whether evidence must be presented in any particular form, and when, to whom and how it should be submitted. Generally, evidence ought to be disclosed in advance to all participants.

3.17 It is critical that parties are not taken by surprise as to what will be considered at a hearing so that they can properly prepare; see further the discussion of the requirements for notice in chapter 2 at paras 2.35–2.40. If allegations have been made against a person, or a decision-maker has specific concerns about that person, fairness is likely to require the decision-maker to ensure that the person is given notice of those allegations or concerns so as to enable them to respond and have their say.

Late evidence and evidence not in a proper form

3.18 Evidence should not be rejected simply because it was not submitted in the correct way, if that will not prejudice the ability of the decision-maker to consider it or the fairness of the process for other affected parties. If evidence is submitted on the day of the hearing when it should have been submitted beforehand, it is not appropriate to reject it out of hand, without considering whether that would be fair. It is better to ask whether or not it would be fair to admit it having regard to:[4]

4 These considerations broadly mirror those for applications for relief from sanctions under r3.5 of the Civil Procedure Rules (CPR).

- how late it has been submitted (there is a major difference, for example, between evidence being submitted a week before the hearing, even if this is later than required, and evidence being submitted on the morning of the hearing itself);
- whether there is any reason why it was submitted late and, if so, how good that reason is;
- how important the evidence is;
- how important the decision is to the party seeking to rely on the evidence (and others affected by the decision); and
- whether any other person affected will be able to respond; if so, whether that would cause any delay; and, if delay would be caused, whether it is fairer to reject the evidence or to adjourn the hearing (on adjournments, see para 3.47 below).

3.19 Technical rules of evidence (for example, the complex rules governing the use of hearsay evidence) do not apply outside of judicial proceedings and it is unlikely to be helpful to resort to technical language. But that does not mean that, for example, a decision-maker cannot have regard to the fact that information is second-hand when considering the weight to give it. It is always open to a decision-maker to decide they will take evidence into account, but to give it less weight if it is thought to be unreliable in some way.

3.20 It may well be appropriate for a decision-maker to admit late evidence but take account of its lateness in the weight given to it. A decision-maker may also decide to admit the evidence on a provisional basis, so that it is considered, but a formal decision whether to admit it and what if any weight to give it is not made until the end of the hearing. (This is still sometimes referred to as admitting evidence '*de bene esse*'.) It is important, however, to ensure that evidence which is considered on this basis is not allowed to influence the decision, even subconsciously, if ultimately it is not formally admitted.

Witnesses

3.21 Sometimes a hearing will require oral evidence from witnesses about factual matters that are in dispute. A person may also want to call witnesses on their behalf to give character evidence. There might also be professionals giving expert evidence. It is a good idea to consider whether, and if so how, witnesses will be enabled to participate in advance of a hearing and to ascertain in advance whether anybody proposes to call a witness and for what purpose. This approach enables effective preparation and time management for a hearing.

3.22 Written witness statements might be requested in advance of the hearing, which may help to reduce the time required for oral representations and give focus to the hearing. Parties may also choose to file witness statements, or there may be a procedural rule requiring any potential witness to file a statement. It is important that the relevant formalities are observed in relation to witness statements, in particular that they are signed and contain a statement of truth.[5]

3.23 If witnesses are to be called, consideration should be given as to whether any limit is appropriate on the time for which any one person can speak, to ensure an orderly hearing. Witness evidence is likely to be particularly important if there are disputed questions of fact to which a witness can speak directly. It may be appropriate to confine the issues in respect of which a particular witness can give evidence. For example, a person may be able to give evidence as to what they have seen and heard, but not have the qualification to offer an expert opinion on a particular issue.

Examination and cross-examination

3.24 If witnesses are called, it is for the decision-maker to decide how they should give their evidence, provided that decision is fair. In some situations, a witness may simply be invited to make a statement. In others, a witness may be asked questions by the decision-maker and/or other participants. Hearing evidence from a live witness provides a good opportunity for a decision-maker to elicit information. It will be important to have regard to any vulnerability or disability which a particular witness may have when considering how they should be invited to give evidence. Guidance on these issues is available in the *Equal Treatment Bench Book* which is available online.[6]

3.25 Cross-examination is the putting of questions, by party B or their representative, to witnesses giving evidence for party A. Whether cross-examination should be permitted will depend on a number of factors, including the issue at stake, the evidence a particular witness has given and any vulnerability the witness may have that might

5 The current form of the statement of truth required by the CPR is as follows: 'I believe that the facts stated in this witness statement are true. I understand that proceedings for contempt of court may be brought against anyone who makes, or causes to be made, a false statement in a document verified by a statement of truth without an honest belief in its truth.' CPR Practice Direction 22 para 2.2.

6 Judicial College, 2024 edition available at www.judiciary.uk/guidance-and-resources/equal-treatment-bench-book-new-2024-edition/

render cross-examination inappropriate. Where the evidence of a particular witness goes to a matter of fact of fundamental importance and is adverse to a particular person's case, fairness may require that the affected person be given the opportunity to test that evidence by cross-examination. That is particularly likely to be the case where the witness is making an allegation of some form of negligence or wrongdoing against the affected person.

3.26 Where a witness is called to give evidence it may amount to procedural unfairness not to allow them to be cross-examined.[7] However, where cross-examination of some witnesses is permitted, this does not necessarily mean that fairness requires that every witness be cross-examined.[8]

3.27 The decision-maker should retain control of the process of giving evidence. It is important to remember that the purpose of cross-examination is to enable a witness' evidence to be tested, and not to enable someone to bully the witness. That is particularly important when dealing with vulnerable witnesses. In some cases, it may be appropriate to invite a person who might be affected by the decision to be taken to submit questions to the decision-maker, for the decision-maker themself to ask of the witness or otherwise prevent a direct confrontation between the affected person and their representative and the witness.

3.28 The decision-maker may want to ask their own questions in the course of, or after, cross-examination and to give the person on whose behalf the witness has been called an opportunity to re-examine the witness (that is, ask further questions) on any matters arising out of the cross-examination.

3.29 Some tribunals will have their own rules about the circumstances in which cross-examination is permitted and the mechanism by which questions will be put to witnesses.

3.30 Generally, in more formal hearings and particularly where parties are legally represented, it is expected that if the evidence of a witness is to be criticised in closing submissions, those criticisms should have been put to them first in cross-examination so the witness has an opportunity to respond.

7 *Loutfi v General Medical Council* [2010] EWHC 1762 (Admin).

8 *Brent LBC v London Regional Passengers Committee* (1985) Financial Times, November 29, CA.

Recording the evidence

3.31 It is important that a clear note is taken of the evidence given to a decision-maker. While this does not necessarily require a verbatim transcript, where evidence is taken from witnesses it is good practice to record both the question asked and the answer given to avoid any doubt as to what has been said. It may be useful to have a dedicated note taker, if practical. In some circumstances, proceedings may be recorded, but participants should be informed if that is going to be the case.

People who may require additional support

3.32 Some people involved in the hearing – those who are taking part because they are affected by the decision or those giving evidence – may require additional support to be able to participate effectively. This may be, for example, because they have a disability or they do not speak English fluently. Where a person's involvement in the hearing is essential or desirable, but they would not be able to take part effectively without such support, fairness requires that they are provided with reasonably necessary assistance. This is also likely to be required to avoid a breach of the Equality Act 2010 (see chapter 5).

Vulnerable people and witnesses

3.33 The decision-maker should be alert throughout the process to the possibility that someone involved in the hearing, either as a party or a witness, ought to be considered vulnerable. Individual personal factors (for example, age, incapacity, impairment or medical condition), environmental factors, or a combination of the two, can give rise to vulnerability. A person may be vulnerable in one context, such as the unfamiliar experience of appearing at a formal hearing, but may not be vulnerable in a context with which they are familiar, such as at work or school. Children and young people – that is, persons under the age of 18 – should be automatically regarded as vulnerable.

3.34 If the decision-maker considers that a person involved in the hearing is vulnerable, they should go on to consider what measures may be taken for that person to take part in the hearing effectively and without causing unnecessary distress. The Advocate's Gateway[9] is an independent body run by a volunteer management committee

9 www.theadvocatesgateway.org/

which provides free access to practical, evidence-based guidance on vulnerable witnesses and defendants in the court system. In particular, their guidance on vulnerable witnesses and parties in the civil courts may be of use to decision-makers in this situation.

Disabilities and health conditions

3.35 It is important for the decision-maker to find out well in advance of the hearing whether anyone who is due to take part, either as someone affected by the decision or as a witness, requires support or adjustments to be made due to a disability. For example:

- mobility issues may require the hearing to be held in a venue with step-free access and suitably sized rooms and internal access;
- adjustments to the procedure used for other witnesses may be required to ensure that a person with learning difficulties is able to give their best evidence;
- visual impairment may require the documents to be used for the hearing to be presented in a format that is, or can be, intelligible to the person concerned, such as through use of a screen reader;
- the hearing may need to be held at a certain time of day and/or in sessions of not longer than a certain length of time to accommodate the needs of a person with chronic pain;
- a person with a learning disability may require documents to be provided in Easy Read format; and
- an autistic person may not understand questions which use complex analogies.

Interpreters

3.36 Where a person requests an interpreter, they should generally be permitted to use one, unless the request is clearly unreasonable (for example, there is clear evidence English is that person's main language and no evidence to suggest the person is unable to understand and communicate in spoken English). Fairness may require that a decision-maker arrange for an interpreter in some circumstances, and a failure to do so may well result in unlawful discrimination, for example, on grounds of race or disability. For example, if a decision vitally affects the interests of a vulnerable person who cannot arrange their own interpreter and cannot meaningfully participate in the proceedings without an interpreter, then it may very well be unfair to proceed without arranging for one.

3.37 It is legitimate for the decision-maker to make inquiries to ensure that the interpreter is appropriately qualified. In some cases, a person may rely on a family member or a friend as an interpreter. There is nothing wrong with that in principle, but the decision-maker should be careful to ensure that the person who is interpreting understands that when providing a translation it is their duty to interpret what has been said faithfully rather than to engage in advocacy. In other words, the interpreter must be told that their only role is to interpret the questions and answers, not to try to assist the person for whom they are interpreting in any way or better explain their answers.

3.38 It may be appropriate to raise the question whether a person needs an interpreter even though they have not requested one if it becomes apparent to a decision-maker that they are struggling to engage with the process by reason of a language barrier. In these situations, the decision-maker should raise the issue sensitively. However, it is ultimately the responsibility of every decision-maker to ensure that their hearing is fair, which means intervening to check the position if it appears that a party or a witness is not able properly to participate in the proceedings on their own.

Representation

3.39 Whether a person should be allowed to be legally represented at a hearing is again a question for the decision-maker to ask themself, but there are circumstances in which fairness will require this. Whether fairness requires that a person be allowed a legal representative will depend on factors including:

- the legal or factual complexity of the case;
- the importance of the issue for the individual concerned;
- whether the individual has the capacity to present their own case; and
- whether legal representation is needed to ensure equality of arms (for example, it is highly likely to be unfair to deny one party legal representation if the other party is legally represented).

3.40 If a party wishes to be legally represented at a hearing, it is likely to be necessary to have a good reason to refuse this request – if only to avoid a fairness challenge to the resulting decision.[10]

10 See eg *Kumar v Hillingdon LBC* [2020] EWHC 3326 (Admin), where the High Court held that parents in dispute with a local authority over an education, health and care plan were entitled to bring a lawyer to a mediation, and this did not require the consent of the local authority or independent mediator.

3.41 Where the decision involves representations on matters of law or policy or handling of witnesses, the case for allowing legal representation will be particularly strong. Similarly, where the hearing is convened to hear allegations against a particular individual, that will be a factor pointing in favour of allowing legal representation to assist that individual (and then all parties should be entitled to have legal representation to ensure 'equality of arms': see further below). In general, it is better to err on the side of permitting an individual to have a legal representative if they want one. However, the fact that an individual has a legal representative does not mean that the decision-maker should cede control over how the hearing is conducted or allow the hearing to become unduly formal or technical.

3.42 It is also important to consider whether legal representation is needed to ensure equality of arms between those involved. If one person is permitted to have a legal representative, then generally the other involved person(s) should be given the same opportunity. But equality of arms may require an individual to be permitted to engage a legal representative even if the other party does not do so – for example, where a case against an individual will be presented by an official with expertise or experience in the matters under consideration, or in participating in such hearings.

3.43 Sometimes, an individual may want to be represented or assisted by a non-lawyer. Again, in principle, it is better to err on the side of permitting an individual to make use of such assistance than not, while remembering that the decision-maker retains control of the proceedings and can take steps to prevent such a representative from acting inappropriately. In judicial decision-making, there are rules as to who can represent individuals in certain courts and tribunals, but these will not apply to other forms of decision-making.

Virtual hearings

3.44 As a result of the COVID-19 pandemic, many hearings which would previously have taken place in person began to take place by video conference or phone conference. Even in the absence of restrictions on social movement, virtual hearings may provide an alternative method of hearing that is more convenient to the parties, especially where, for example, parties would need to travel long distances to attend an in-person hearing. The choice between a virtual and an in-person hearing is not a binary one: it may be the case that some participants in the hearing are physically present in the same room as each other, while others attend via video conference or phone. These hearings are often referred to as 'hybrid' hearings.

3.45 As a starting point, *all* of the factors outlined in this chapter apply to virtual hearings in more or less the same manner as they apply to in-person hearings. But virtual hearings present their own particular considerations which should be carefully thought through and applied to the particular case if you propose to hold a hearing virtually, either in whole or in part.

Virtual hearing checklist

3.46 The following checklist should help you to decide when it is appropriate to hold a hearing virtually and to run a virtual hearing smoothly in the event that you do so.

Checklist

- Will all parties be able to participate fully, fairly and properly in the hearing if it is held virtually, rather than in person? If any parties would be put at a material disadvantage because the hearing is held virtually, it will almost certainly be better to hold an in-person hearing, unless there are countervailing factors pointing against this. In particular, it is helpful to ask questions such as:
  - Does every party have access to the necessary technology to participate in the hearing and the ability to use that technology?
  - Will any additional support that a person requires be capable of being provided remotely?
  - If the hearing is held remotely, will every party have access to all the evidence and materials that are being considered?
- Should the hearing be held entirely virtually, or can some participants appear in person rather than remotely? For example, you might hold the hearing entirely virtually, save for a particular individual who would be unable to participate fairly and properly without being heard in person. Or you might hold the hearing entirely in person, save for a particular individual who lives a long way from the venue or is self-isolating due to a medical condition. In the latter situation, it is particularly important to ensure that the remote hearing arrangements are

fair to that individual, who will be physically distanced from the other participants and the decision-maker.

- In the event that you do decide to hold the hearing virtually, it is almost always best for the decision-maker to host the hearing, and to dedicate a member of staff who is not part of the hearing panel to handling the administrative aspects of this, such as admitting persons to the conference, helping with technical difficulties, and so on.
- Decide on whether the hearing will be heard by way of video conference or phone conference. In the event that you decide to use video conference, you should check with all parties that they will be able to access the platform that you use (for example, Microsoft Teams, Zoom, Cisco WebEx, and so on). In most cases, to join the video conference as a guest, participants should need no more than a webcam-enabled computer or laptop and access to a web browser.
- Make sure that well in advance of the hearing, you distribute to all parties the details to access the hearing, including:
  - the start time and date. It is usually advisable to require parties to join the conference at least 15 minutes prior to the start, or require them to join at a specific time (for example, an hour in advance) to test their connection with support staff;
  - the dial-in number, for a phone conference;
  - a link to the web address, for a video conference;
  - any security code, meeting code or ID, and so on;
  - the contact details for parties to contact in the event of technical issues during the hearing; and
  - for a video conference, also ask all parties to confirm that they have access to a strong and fast internet connection.
- Ideally, and especially for a video conference, organise a short test-run with all parties a day or two before the hearing, so that any technological issues can be identified early and resolved.
- Parties should be reminded that although the hearing is being heard virtually, it remains a formal hearing and they should observe the same level of courtesy, formality, dress code, and so on, as they would for an in-person hearing. It is particularly important in a virtual hearing (video conference or phone conference) for participants to avoid speaking over one another.

- Before the hearing, parties should be advised to ensure that, during the hearing, they will be in a quiet room, free from interruptions and, if appropriate, on their own. At the start of the hearing (and, if necessary, during the hearing), ask all parties who are not currently speaking to mute their microphones, to reduce feedback.
- In certain cases, you may wish to ask a remote participant to confirm that they are alone or who else is present in the room with them (who may not be visible via webcam).
- Documents:
  - Documentary evidence can be trickier to deal with when people do not have access to hard copies. It is usually advisable to insist all documents that parties wish to rely on are submitted in PDF format, so that they will appear identically to everyone present. You may need to set up a document sharing platform (such as Dropbox) if the files submitted are too large to be emailed to everyone.
  - Most video conference platforms allow parties to share their screen so that it can be seen by other participants. This can be useful for parties to refer to relevant documents. As host, you will normally be able to control whether participants have permission to share their screens.
  - You should be prepared to consider permitting a party to submit a previously unsubmitted document during the hearing by way of email, in the same way as you would consider permitting such a party to hand up a physical copy of such a document at an in-person hearing.
- Consider whether to record or transcribe the hearing and, if so, how. For video conferences, most platforms permit the host to make a recording of the video and audio.
- Just as with other hearings (see above, at para 3.9 onwards) a virtual hearing may be public or private. Where the decision is taken to hold some or all of a virtual hearing in public, consideration may need to be given to how members of the public can access the hearing (for example, by providing an email address which people can contact in order to obtain the login details for the hearing). If members of the public are in attendance, the decision-maker may need to explain at the outset that they should remain on mute and are not permitted to interrupt the proceedings.

Adjournments

3.47 Parties to a decision may want the decision or hearing to be delayed for any number of reasons – unavailability of witnesses, needing more time to produce documentary evidence, ill health, or a delay in finding legal representation. Each request will need to be considered on its facts, but there are some general principles that it will be helpful to bear in mind.

Overall duration of the decision-making process

3.48 Always bear in mind the overall duration of the decision-making process. Where someone's reputation or career is threatened, or where the decision will have a direct impact on their personal life, for example, the provision of support services, it is important to make sure that decisions are made promptly and efficiently. If adjournments are required, ensure that they are for the shortest time that is reasonable, and that everyone is very clear about what the purpose of the adjournment is, so that the matter will be ready to be decided on the next occasion.

Legal advice/representation

3.49 If someone wants to have legal representation at a hearing, or to take legal advice, it will usually be appropriate to give them this opportunity, particularly where the decision will have a significant impact on their personal life, for example, their career or their access to services. This is particularly true where the other person affected by the decision already has the benefit of legal advice or representation. The fundamental principle of equality of arms is relevant. (See paras 3.39–3.43 above.)

Absence due to ill-health

3.50 If someone is so unwell they cannot attend and take part in the hearing, and their involvement in the decision is critical – whether because they will be directly affected by the decision or because they have important evidence to give which cannot be obtained in any other way – it will usually be appropriate to re-schedule the decision or hearing to accommodate them. It is generally not unreasonable to ask for evidence of ill-health, such as a letter from a general practitioner, particularly if the adjournment requested is unusually long. However, there may be exceptional circumstances where such evidence cannot reasonably be obtained in the required timeframe, and the decision-maker will have to 'do their best' to reach a fair decision on whether to adjourn.

More time to present evidence

3.51 If someone wants an adjournment so that they may have more time to present evidence, it is not unreasonable to ask whether there are any particular reasons why they have not been able to gather the evidence on time for the hearing or to insist on a clear timetable within which the evidence will be obtained.

All necessary evidence and information is submitted before decision

3.52 It is important that decision-makers do not take a decision until they are sure they have all the evidence and information they need. If that means a short delay to obtain further information, it is likely to save time in the long run to permit a short adjournment, with clear instructions about what is to happen before the re-scheduled hearing or panel meeting.

CHAPTER 4

Making a decision

continued

4.1 This chapter summarises the legal principles that apply to decisions made by public bodies. Some of them may also be relevant to private bodies, for example, the need to give reasons for a decision. We would suggest that private bodies will generally want to ensure their decisions comply with the minimum requirements of 'public law' set out in this chapter, even though there may not be a strict legal obligation for them to do so.

Acting within your powers

The key principle

4.2 A public body must act within the scope of its powers. A failure to do so will be an error of law.[1] This is sometimes described as the '*vires*' principle, and a decision taken outside of the scope of a public body's powers is sometimes described as an '*ultra vires*' decision.

The distinction between a power and a duty

4.3 If a public body is subject to a duty, it must comply with that duty. A duty will generally be imposed by the use of mandatory language, for example, 'must' or 'must not', 'shall' or 'shall not'.

4.4 If a public body has a power to act, then it will be for the public body to decide whether or not to act. That is often referred to as a 'discretion'. A failure by a public body to consider exercising a relevant power in appropriate circumstances will usually be an error of law.

4.5 The key distinction between duties and powers is that a power need not be exercised, but a duty must be discharged.[2]

4.6 Where a public body has a power, it will usually be unlawful to 'fetter' the exercise of that power by adopting an over-rigid policy.

1 The classic definition of illegality was given by Lord Diplock in *Council of Civil Service Unions v Minister for the Civil Service* [1985] AC 374, HL at 410 when he said:

> By 'illegality' as a ground for judicial review I mean that the decision-maker must understand correctly the law that regulates his decision-making power and must give effect to it. Whether he has or not is par excellence a justiciable question to be decided, in the event of dispute, by those persons, the judges, by whom the judicial power of the state is exercisable.

2 See Lord Nicholls in *R (G) v Barnet LBC* [2003] UKHL 57 at [12].

The source of powers and duties

4.7 It is important to be aware of the source of the powers and duties that a public body may have. In many cases, a public body is created by statute and such powers as it has come from the statute which created it or another relevant statute. Public bodies may also have powers deriving from the common law or contract. The powers of private bodies will normally be set out in the document establishing the body, for example, the articles of association.

Interpreting provisions conferring powers and imposing duties

4.8 If a public body misinterprets the scope of its powers, this can make the resulting decision unlawful.[3]

4.9 It is not always the case that the words 'must' and 'may' neatly indicate duties and powers respectively.[4] Other language may also be used. For example, a public body may have a duty to take reasonable steps to do something. In that case, what steps are reasonable will be for the public body to determine, having regard to the scope of its powers to take relevant steps. The decision as to what steps are reasonable could only be challenged if it was itself irrational, ie outside the range of reasonable decisions open to the decision-maker (see para 4.50 onwards below).

4.10 Another example is the use of the word 'should', which is frequently used in statutory guidance. 'Should' often means something between 'may' and 'must'; for example, it may mean that a public body should do something unless there is a particularly good reason not to. However, the use of 'should' in guidance cannot by itself create a legal duty to do something. For this reason, some stat-

3 For example, in *Bromley LBC v Greater London Council* [1983] 1 AC 768, HL, the House of Lords held that the Greater London Council had misunderstood its powers under the Transport (London) Act 1969 when it issued a precept requiring the London boroughs to levy a supplementary rate to enable the GLC to make a grant to the London Transport Executive to reduce the cost of bus and tube fares.

4 For example, in *M v Scottish Ministers* [2012] UKSC 58, certain provisions of the Mental Health (Care and Treatment) (Scotland) Act 2003 were to come into force on such date as the Scottish ministers 'may' appoint. That conferred a power to make an order for the provisions to come into force; but it was unlawful not to exercise that power since that would frustrate the purposes of the statute.

utory guidance[5] uses the word 'must' in bold when it seeks to explain legal duties, and the word 'should' in ordinary text when it is encouraging a person to take a particular course but without there being a legal requirement to do so.

Implied powers

4.11 A public body may have powers that are implied, as well as those that are expressly set out in the relevant legislation.

4.12 For example, the court will often be willing to imply that a public body has powers 'incidental' to or consequential upon the express power, where that is necessary for it to perform its express statutory functions.[6] The test is one of necessity: the fact that a power may be sensible or desirable in order to perform the primary power does not mean that a public body has it.[7]

4.13 Sometimes, a statute will confer powers in very general terms. For example, section 1 of the Localism Act 2011 provides a local authority 'has power to do anything that individuals generally may do'.

The conditions for the exercise of a power or duty

4.14 A power may be conferred or duty imposed subject to a statutory precondition as to the existence of certain facts, or requirement that the decision-maker judges that a certain state of affairs has arisen. It will always be for the court to decide on the meaning of the statutory language. If a public body interprets the provision incorrectly then that will be an error of law and its decision can be quashed.

4.15 Once the legal meaning has been determined, the question will arise whether, in the real world, the conditions for the exercise of a power or duty are satisfied. That means considering whether a certain state of affairs exists as a matter of fact; and may also mean applying an evaluative judgment to that state of affairs. Often, the courts will consider that findings of fact and matters of evaluation are for the public body to decide subject only to review on grounds such

5 See eg Department for Education and Department of Health and Social Care *SEND code of practice: 0 to 25 years* (April 2014, last updated April 2020).

6 See eg *Attorney General v Great Eastern Railway Co* (1880) 5 App Cas 473 at 478.

7 See eg *Ward v Commissioner of Police of the Metropolis* [2005] UKHL 32 at [24] and *McCarthy & Stone (Developments) Ltd v Richmond upon Thames LBC* [1992] 2 AC 48, HL, in which the House of Lords held that the London Borough of Richmond did not have power to charge for the use of a discretionary planning advisory service that it offered.

as irrationality (on which see para 4.50 below). But sometimes the court will consider that it should determine such matters for itself where there is a dispute.[8]

4.16 Sometimes, a power may be conferred subject to the decision-maker holding a particular belief.[9] Where a power is subject to a precondition, whether a matter of precedent fact or evaluation, it is important for the decision-maker to apply their mind to the question whether that precondition is satisfied and it is good practice to ensure that this is properly recorded, with reasons.

Implied restriction on powers

4.17 An apparently unfettered power or discretion will generally be subject to a number of implied restrictions on its exercise. The following are some of the important restrictions that the courts will generally imply.

4.18 A power or duty must be exercised reasonably, having regard to relevant considerations and without having regard to irrelevant considerations.[10] This is considered in more detail at para 4.50 below.

4.19 A power or duty does not authorise a breach of common law 'constitutional rights' unless by way of necessary implication or clear words to that effect[11] (this is known as the 'principle of legality'). There is no exhaustive list of 'constitutional rights', nor is the scope of such rights necessarily settled. Constitutional rights are not necessarily absolute and may conflict with one another. If the question arose whether the exercise of a power would interfere with a constitutional right it is likely to be prudent to take legal advice.

4.20 The following are potential 'constitutional rights' that may be of relevance to decision-makers:

- the right to life;[12]
- the right not to be tortured;[13]

8 For example, the question of whether a person is a 'child' for the purposes of the Children Act 1989 is a question for the court to resolve for itself, not merely reviewing whether the decision-maker has reached a reasonable decision on this question: *R (A) v Croydon LBC* [2009] UKSC 8.

9 See eg *R v Rochester City Council ex p Hobday* (1989) 58 P & CR 424, QBD.

10 See eg *R v Tower Hamlets LBC ex p Chetnik Developments Ltd* [1988] AC 858, HL at 872.

11 See eg *R v Secretary of State for the Home Department ex p Simms* [2000] 2 AC 115, HL.

12 *R (Amin) v Secretary of State for the Home Department* [2003] UKHL 51.

13 *A v Secretary of State for the Home Department (No 2)* [2005] UKHL 71.

- the right not to be condemned to a life so destitute that no civilised nation can tolerate it;[14]
- the right not to be detained arbitrarily;[15]
- the right of access to justice.[16] It is a matter of particular concern to the courts that there be effective access to justice;
- the right to a fair hearing;[17]
- the right against self-incrimination;[18]
- the right not to be subject to unauthorised restrictions on freedom of movement;[19]
- the right to freedom of expression;[20]
- the right of peaceful assembly;[21] and
- the right not to be expropriated of property.[22]

4.21 There is a presumption against defeating statutory rights.[23] Where Parliament has conferred a right upon somebody, it is generally presumed that a power should not be exercised so as to breach that right unless it is clear that this is permissible.

The duty to consider the exercise of a power

4.22 Where a public body has a power to do something, it will generally be obliged to consider whether to exercise that power where an appropriate situation arises. The circumstances in which that duty is triggered will depend on the particular context. For example, some powers may fall to be exercised only if there is a complaint or an application or request.[24] In other cases, the public body may have a duty proactively to consider the exercise of a power even where it has not been asked to do so. Where there is an ongoing power to act, the

14 *R v Secretary of State for Social Security ex p Joint Council for the Welfare of Immigrants* [1997] 1 WLR 275, CA.

15 *A v Secretary of State for the Home Department* [2004] UKHL 56.

16 *R (Unison) v Lord Chancellor* [2017] UKSC 51.

17 *R (McCann) v Manchester Crown Court* [2002] UKHL 39.

18 *R v Director of Serious Fraud Office ex p Smith* [1993] AC 1, HL.

19 *R (W) v Commissioner of Police of the Metropolis* [2006] EWCA Civ 458.

20 *McCartan Turkington Breen v Times Newspapers Ltd* [2001] 2 AC 277, HL (NI).

21 *DPP v Jones* [1999] 2 AC 240, HL.

22 *R (Sainsbury's Supermarkets Ltd) v Wolverhampton City Council* [2010] UKSC 20.

23 See eg *R v Secretary of State for Social Security ex p Joint Council for the Welfare of Immigrants* (1997) 1 WLR 275, CA.

24 See eg *Threadneedle Property Investments Ltd v Southwark LBC* [2012] EWHC 855 (Admin).

public body will have to keep under consideration the question whether or not to exercise that power from time to time.[25]

The prohibition on fettering discretion conferred by statute

4.23 Where a power is conferred on a public body by statute, it may not 'fetter' the exercise of that power.

4.24 A public body may not fetter its discretion by adopting an over-rigid policy as to whether or not it will exercise the power or as to the circumstances in which it will exercise the power.[26] There will be a balance to be struck between, on the one hand, the desirability of adopting a policy to ensure consistency and predictability in decision-making, and, on the other, the need to avoid a policy being formulated or applied in an over-rigid manner. Note that both the formulation of the policy and its operation are important: a public body that operates a policy which, on its face, permits exceptions may nonetheless be acting unlawfully if, in practice, the policy is operated rigidly.

4.25 A public body cannot fetter its discretion with regard to its statutory powers by contract. It cannot bind itself not to exercise a statutory power, or to exercise it only in a certain way, by contracting with another.

No abdication of powers

4.26 A public body cannot abdicate its power of decision to another person. There is nothing wrong with a public body having regard to the opinion or decision of another body and consulting as appropriate, but it must retain the ultimate power of decision.

No delegation without authority

4.27 A public body charged with the exercise of a public function may not delegate that function to another body, unless it is expressly or impliedly authorised to do so.[27] Generally, the more important the function and the greater the margin of discretion, the less likely that

25 *R v Secretary of State for the Home Department ex p Fire Brigades Union* [1995] 2 AC 513, HL.

26 See eg *British Oxygen Co Ltd v Minister of Technology* [1971] AC 610, HL.

27 See eg *Audit Commission v Ealing LBC* [2005] EWCA Civ 556.

there will be an implied power to delegate, whereas the closer the function is to a purely administrative function, the greater the likelihood that a power to delegate will be implied.[28] The nature and extent of the purported delegation is also important. For example, it is more likely to be permissible to delegate the function of gathering or analysing information in order to inform the decision-maker than to delegate the making of the decision itself.[29]

4.28 Where a duty or power is conferred on a statutory office-holder, there is a presumption that parliament intends the officer to exercise the power personally.[30] However, where the duties attaching to such an office are so numerous that it would be impossible for them all to be exercised personally, there may conversely arise a presumption that there is a power to delegate.[31]

4.29 Where there is a power to delegate, it is important to be clear to whom the exercise of the power is delegated; when, and in what circumstances, the power is being delegated; and what the scope of the delegation is. These matters should be recorded in writing to minimise the risk of doubt or dispute as to what has been delegated. Where power has been delegated, generally the person to whom it is delegated cannot delegate the power further.[32]

Is there a power to reconsider a decision?

4.30 It sometimes happens that a public body takes a decision but then wants to re-take the decision, perhaps because fresh information has arisen or perhaps because the decision-maker has changed their mind about what they should have decided. But a decision-maker does not necessarily have the power to re-take a decision. Where a decision-maker does not have the power to re-take a decision, it is sometimes said to be '*functus officio*'.[33]

4.31 The question whether a decision-maker does not have power to re-take a decision depends on the particular legal framework to which

28 Compare eg *Vine v National Dock Labour Board* [1957] AC 488, HL and *R v Monopolies and Mergers Commission ex p Argyll Group plc* [1986] 1 WLR 763, CA.

29 See eg *R v Race Relations Board ex p Selvarajan* [1975] 1 WLR 1686, CA; *R v Managers of South Western Hospital ex p M* [1993] QB 683, QBD.

30 *R v Chief Constable of Greater Manchester Police ex p Lainton* [2000] ICR 1324, CA.

31 *DPP v Haw* [2007] EWHC 1931 (Admin).

32 *Barnard v National Dock Labour Board* [1953] 2 QB 18, CA.

33 *Re 56 Denton Road, Twickenham* [1953] Ch 51, ChD.

it owes its power of decision. For example, where a decision-maker has to make a decision on a particular individual application, it is likely that once it has reached a decision on that application it cannot be re-taken. That is because of the importance of certainty and finality in decision-making to good administration. It might be different if the individual affected consents to the decision being re-taken, but that will depend on the particular circumstances.

4.32 Of course, it may be possible for an individual to make a further application which could be considered afresh. There may also be a power to review or reconsider a decision. For example, where a local authority owes an ongoing duty to provide support to a child or adult, it will generally be open to the local authority to review that support in line with the statutory framework.

4.33 Sometimes, though, even where both the individual affected and the decision-maker agree that a decision should be set aside and reconsidered, they will have no choice but to apply to the Administrative Court to quash the decision. This can be done where appropriate with the consent of the decision-maker.

Improper motive

The key principle

4.34 A public body must only use a statutory power for its proper purpose. If a power is used for any unauthorised purpose (an 'improper' purpose), the public body will act unlawfully.[34] A public body may also act unlawfully when it decides for an improper purpose *not* to exercise a statutory power.[35]

4.35 The test for improper purposes is simply whether the public body has acted for the purpose authorised by the legislation.

Identifying purposes

4.36 The courts will determine in each case: (a) the purpose of a particular statute; and (b) the purpose for which the powers were in fact used by the public body.

4.37 The legislation will sometimes expressly state the purpose or purposes for which powers are to be used. In this situation, the

34 *Porter v Magill* [2001] UKHL 67 at [19].

35 *Padfield v Minister of Agriculture, Fisheries and Food* [1968] AC 997, HL.

decision-maker may only act for the stated purposes. Where the scope of the stated purposes is unclear, it will be a matter for the courts to interpret the legislation to find out the scope of the conferred powers.[36]

4.38 An important principle of statutory interpretation is that courts will presume that parliament intends powers to be used in a way that promotes the policy and objects of the legislation.[37]

4.39 Often, however, legislation does not expressly state the purposes for which powers are to be used. In this situation, decision-makers and the courts have to interpret the legislation to ascertain the implied purposes of the powers.

4.40 Ascertaining the purpose for which powers were in fact used is a question of fact. The court will consider all of the circumstances, and will not always accept at face value the reasons put forward by the public body as to why it exercised a particular power. A court may take into account the surrounding circumstances.[38]

Multiple purposes

4.41 A public body might act for more than one purpose when it exercises a statutory power. In this situation the key test is whether the public body's 'main' or 'dominant' purpose was the one authorised by the statute.[39]

4.42 A public body must not exercise its powers in bad faith.[40] Even where a public body's dominant purpose is authorised by the statute, the decision will be unlawful if any of its other purposes involve bad faith.

4.43 The following are examples of where a public body exercised its powers for an improper purpose, in different areas of decision-making. However, it is important to remember that the question of

36 See eg *R (Coughlan) v Minister for the Cabinet Office* [2022] UKSC 11 at [50]–[52], [77] and *R (Elliott-Smith) v Secretary of State for Business, Energy and Industrial Strategy* [2021] EWHC 1633 (Admin) at [66]–[67] and [73]–[74].

37 *Padfield v Minister of Agriculture, Fisheries and Food* [1968] AC 997, HL at 1030, 1045, 1053–1054.

38 See eg *Webb v Minister of Housing and Local Government* [1965] 1 WLR 755, CA at 777.

39 See eg *R (Trafford) v Blackpool BC* [2014] EWHC 85 (Admin) at [71]; *R (Richards) v Pembrokeshire CC* [2004] EWCA Civ 1000 at [44]. See also *Webb v Minister of Housing and Local Government* [1965] 1 WLR 755, CA at 778 and *R v Ealing LBC ex p Times Newspapers Ltd* (1987) 85 LGR 316, DC at 326.

40 See eg *Anisminic Ltd v Foreign Compensation Commission* [1969] 2 AC 147, HL at 171.

what purposes are improper is a question that requires specific consideration of the statutory context in issue.

Landlord and tenant

4.44 A local authority acted for an improper purpose when it used its power to refuse to renew a lease in order to get revenge against a solicitor.[41]

Compulsory purchase

4.45 A public body acted for an improper purpose when it exercised a power to make a compulsory purchase order relating to coastal protection for the purpose of building a promenade for public amenity.[42]

Housing

4.46 A public body acted for an improper purpose when it used a power to dispose of housing stock to promote the electoral advantage of the dominant party on the council.[43]

Related principles

4.47 It is unlawful for a public body to exercise a statutory power in a way that frustrates the policy or objects of the legislation.[44] This principle focuses on the outcome of the public body's decision, rather than on its purposes for acting in a certain way. Nevertheless, the two principles are closely related and could both arise in relation to a decision.

4.48 Furthermore, when a public body uses its powers for an improper purpose, it also risks breaching the separate principle that public bodies must not take into account irrelevant considerations. The courts have noted the overlap between the two principles on a number of occasions, and sometimes the distinction between the two principles can be hard to identify.[45] The irrelevant considerations principle is considered at para 4.63 onwards below.

41 *R (Trafford) v Blackpool BC* [2014] EWHC 85 (Admin).

42 *Webb v Minister of Housing and Local Government* [1965] 1 WLR 755, CA.

43 *Porter v Magill* [2001] UKHL 67.

44 See eg *JP Whitter (Waterwell Engineers) Ltd v Revenue and Customs Commissioners* [2018] UKSC 31 at [21].

45 See eg *R v Secretary of State for Foreign and Commonwealth Affairs ex p World Development Movement Ltd* [1995] 1 WLR 386, DC at 401.

Rationality

Introduction

4.49 Decision-makers are required to make rational decisions. Decisions can be irrational in two ways, which are often linked. First, a decision can be irrational because it is outside the range of reasonable decisions open to the decision-maker.[46] Second, a decision can be irrational because of a flaw in the process by which it was taken – for example, that significant reliance was placed on an irrelevant consideration, or that there was no evidence to support an important step in the reasoning, or that the reasoning involved a serious logical or methodological error.[47]

Irrationality/unreasonableness standard

4.50 'Irrationality' in this context is also often referred to as '*Wednesbury* unreasonableness'. That is because the concept originates from a case of that name, in which it was explained that a decision will be unreasonable in public law terms if it is 'so unreasonable that no reasonable [decision-maker] could ever have come to it'.[48] A more modern formulation of the test is whether a decision was 'beyond the range of responses open to a reasonable decision-maker'.[49]

4.51 Regardless of the precise way in which the test is expressed, there is no doubt that it amounts to a very high threshold. What has to be shown is that *no* reasonable decision-maker would have reached the same decision. In other words, the decision must fall outside the scope of reasonable disagreement.

4.52 However, the way in which a court assesses irrationality will vary from case to case. That is because the test involves 'a sliding scale of review, more or less intrusive according to the nature and gravity of what is at stake'.[50] The court will generally apply a particularly rigorous standard of review where a decision interferes with fundamental rights, while less rigorous scrutiny is likely if the decision is a

46 *Boddington v British Transport Police* [1999] 2 AC 143, HL at 175 per Lord Steyn.

47 *R (Law Society) v Lord Chancellor* [2018] EWHC 2094 (Admin) at [98].

48 *Associated Provincial Picture Houses Ltd v Wednesbury Corp* [1948] 1 KB 223, CA at 230 per Lord Greene MR.

49 See eg *R v Ministry of Defence ex p Smith* [1996] QB 517, CA per Sir Thomas Bingham MR.

50 *R v Secretary of State for Education and Employment ex p Begbie* [2000] 1 WLR 1115, CA per Laws LJ.

political judgment and/or the court lacks the experience and expertise of the original decision-maker.[51] A more intense review may also be appropriate in cases where decisions will have a profound impact.[52]

4.53 A stricter standard of rationality, overlapping with proportionality, can be relevant where fundamental or constitutional rights are concerned.[53] – see further chapter 6, Complying with the Human Rights Act 1998.

Examples

Absence of a logical basis for the decision

4.54 The classic example of an irrational/unreasonable decision taught to law students is a decision to dismiss a teacher because they have red hair.[54] Plainly, the colour of a teacher's hair has no rational connection to whether they should remain in post or be dismissed.

4.55 Similarly, decisions where it is not possible to discern the reasoning which led to the decision or where inadequate reasons are given may be irrational/unreasonable. A finding by a police disciplinary tribunal that a police officer had been 'provoked' into racist behaviour was in the context of the panel's other findings so inexplicable as to be irrational.[55]

Errors in approach

4.56 Irrationality/unreasonableness may arise where the decision-maker approaches the making of a decision in a way that cannot be justified. While the weight to be given to any material consideration is a matter for the decision-maker, this is subject to the principle of rationality.[56] For example, a social worker's failure to take into account material evidence about the support required by a severely disabled young person went beyond a disagreement with the views of experts and

51 *Kennedy v Charity Commission* [2014] UKSC 20 at [51]–[55] per Lord Mance.

52 *R (KM, by his mother and litigation friend JM) v Cambridgeshire CC* [2012] UKSC 23.

53 This principle is usually described as 'variable intensity rationality review': see *Pham v Secretary of State for the Home Department* [2015] UKSC 19.

54 *Associated Provincial Picture Houses Ltd v Wednesbury Corp* [1948] 1 KB 223, CA at 229, citing the example given in *Short v Poole Corp* [1926] Ch 66, CA.

55 *R (Chief Constable of the West Midlands) v Police Misconduct Panel* [2020] EWHC 1400 (Admin) at [63].

56 *Secretary of State for the Home Department v AP (No 1)* [2011] [2010] UKSC 24.

carers, and meant that the conclusions of a needs assessment were unlawful.[57]

4.57 Likewise, decisions that are not supported by or undermined by errors as to the evidence may give rise to challenges on this ground. For example, a failure meaningfully to evaluate the claimant's evidence and the possibility of good reasons for an account that changed over time meant that it was irrational to conclude the claimant could not be a victim of trafficking.[58]

Unduly oppressive impact

4.58 A decision may be irrational/unreasonable where it has an unduly oppressive impact on the individual affected. For example, it was considered irrational to revoke a stall-holder's licence for a trivial incident which resulted in the loss of his livelihood.[59]

Discrimination and arbitrariness

4.59 Individuals in similar situations should be treated in a similar way, and decision-makers should act in a broadly consistent manner.[60] Where a decision-maker treats somebody less favourably than another in a comparable situation without proper justification, this runs the risk of being irrational/unreasonable. A decision to exclude mushroom-pickers from a reduced minimum wage for harvesters was held to be unlawful on this basis.[61]

4.60 If the decision engages relevant protected characteristics, it may well also be unlawful under the Equality Act 2010 (see chapter 5) as well as irrational. For example, limiting measures that applied to suspected terrorists only to suspected terrorists with no right of residence in the UK was discriminatory and irrational.[62]

4.61 Equally, if the decision engages a person's human rights, unjustified differences in treatment might breach Article 14 of the European Convention on Human Rights (ECHR) (see chapter 6 at para 6.56 onwards), which prohibits discrimination in the enjoyment of many human rights.

57 *R (JG) v Southwark LBC* [2020] EWHC 1989 (Admin).

58 *R (WEN) v Secretary of State for the Home Department* [2019] EWHC 2104 (Admin) at [62]–[63].

59 *R v Barnsley MBC ex p Hook* [1976] 1 WLR 1052, CA.

60 *R (O'Brien) v Independent Assessor* [2007] UKHL 10 at [30].

61 *R (Middlebrook Mushrooms Ltd) v Agricultural Wages Board of England and Wales* [2004] EWHC 1447 (Admin) at [74].

62 *A v Secretary of State for the Home Department* [2004] UKHL 56.

Pointers for decision-makers

4.62 Rational/reasonable decisions will generally:

- be clearly based on the evidence before the decision-maker;
- only be made once the decision-maker is satisfied that they have the information/evidence necessary to make the decision.[63] If the decision-maker considers that important material is lacking, then this must be obtained before a lawful decision can be made;
- have a logical explanation (a decision is less likely to be found irrational if reasons have been provided and these are adequate);[64]
- have internally consistent reasoning (if a decision contradicts itself then it may well be irrational);
- not have an unduly oppressive impact on the individual affected. This is most likely to be a concern in the context of disciplinary and/or sanctions decisions;
- be consistent with other similar decisions; and
- not be affected by any unjustified assumptions or stereotypes about those involved (such a decision may in event be unlawful for taking into account an irrelevant consideration and/or for being discriminatory).

Relevant and irrelevant considerations

The key principle

4.63 The key principle is that when a public body makes a decision, it must take into account all *relevant considerations,* and must not take into account any irrelevant considerations.

4.64 There are three categories of consideration:

- *Relevant considerations,* which must be taken into account.
- *Irrelevant considerations,* which must not be taken into account.
- Considerations which may be taken into account, sometimes called *permissible considerations.* A public body has a discretion whether to take into account permissible considerations, but must act rationally and must not ignore anything that is obviously material.[65]

63 *Secretary of State for Education and Science v Tameside MBC* [1977] AC 1014, HL.

64 See para 4.107 onwards below.

65 *R (Friends of the Earth Ltd) v Heathrow Airport Ltd* [2020] UKSC 52 at [116]–[121].

First category: Relevant considerations

4.65 A relevant consideration is a factor that a public body must take into account, as identified in legislation or policy. The requirement to take something into account may be either express or implied in the legislation. The courts interpret legislation to determine whether a certain factor is one which the public body must take into account.

4.66 There are many examples of relevant considerations *expressly* identified in legislation. For example:

(1) a public body must have regard to certain specified factors when preparing an adult care and support plan;[66]

(2) when exercising functions under the Education Acts, public bodies are required to have regard to the principle that pupils are to be educated in accordance with the wishes of their parents.[67]

4.67 The test for identifying whether a consideration is *impliedly* identified in legislation is whether the consideration is 'so obviously material' to a decision that failing to consider it would not go against the intention of the legislation.[68]

Evidence as a relevant consideration

4.68 Evidence may also be a relevant consideration that a decision-maker must take into account.[69] This is connected with a public body's duty to make sufficient inquiries to inform itself of all relevant considerations, which is explained further below.

'Weight' attached to relevant consideration

4.69 The weight attached to a relevant consideration is generally a matter for the decision-maker.[70] The courts will only intervene if the public body has acted unreasonably in attaching too much weight to a

66 Care Act 2014 s25.

67 Education Act 1996 s9. See also Children and Families Act 2014 s19, setting out a list of considerations which must be taken into account when a local authority exercises functions in relation to children with special educational needs.

68 *R (Friends of the Earth Ltd) v Heathrow Airport Ltd* [2020] UKSC 52 at [116].

69 *R (National Association of Health Stores) v Secretary of State for Health* [2005] EWCA Civ 154 at [73]–[75].

70 *Tesco Stores Ltd v Secretary of State for the Environment and West Oxfordshire DC* [1995] 1 WLR 759, HL at 780.

particular consideration,[71] or too little.[72] Where legislation states that 'special' or 'particular' regard should be had to a factor, public bodies should usually give most weight to that factor.[73]

Second category: Irrelevant considerations

4.70 An irrelevant consideration is something that a decision-maker must not take into account. The question of whether a consideration is irrelevant is a question of law for the courts.

4.71 To show that a decision unlawfully took into account irrelevant considerations, it is not necessary to show that the irrelevant factor was the main influence on the decision. It is enough to show that the irrelevant factor played a material role in the decision-making. This means that it can be easier for a claimant to show that a decision was unlawful due to irrelevant considerations than to show that a decision was unlawful due to improper purposes (which are considered separately at para 4.34 onwards above).

4.72 Sometimes, legislation states that only certain considerations can be taken into account, or that certain considerations must not be taken into account. In these situations, it is relatively straightforward to identify an irrelevant consideration.

4.73 In other cases, the question of whether a factor is an irrelevant consideration depends on how the court interprets the legislation. This may be the case, for example, where the decision-maker has regard to factors which are not relevant to the legislative purpose. In deciding what considerations to take into account, public bodies should consider the purpose of the legislation, and whether considering certain factors would be consistent with that legislative purpose.

Third category: Permissible considerations

4.74 The third category concerns considerations that are not expressly or impliedly identified in the statute or policy. Except where the consideration is one that is so obviously material that it must be taken into account, the public body has a discretion as to whether to take such factors into account, provided that it acts rationally.[74]

71 See eg *R (Gallagher) v Basildon DC* [2010] EWHC 2824 (Admin) at [41].
72 *R v Mid Hertfordshire Justices ex p Cox* (1996) 8 Admin LR 409, QBD at 413H.
73 See eg *R (Garner) v Elmbridge BC* [2011] EWCA Civ 891 at [4] and [8]; *R (Mehanne) v Westminster Housing Benefit Review Board* [2001] UKHL 11 at [13].
74 *R (Friends of the Earth Ltd) v Heathrow Airport Ltd* [2020] UKSC 52 at [116].

Examples

4.75 Whether a consideration is relevant, irrelevant or permissible depends heavily on the language and context of the legislation in question. This needs to be kept in mind when considering examples from different legislative contexts. With this word of caution in mind, some examples are provided here to give a flavour of the type of considerations that public bodies should and should not take into account.

Public sector equality duty

4.76 In exercising their functions, public bodies must have regard to a series of needs, including (i) the need to eliminate discrimination, and (ii) the need to advance equality of opportunity.[75] See further chapter 5 at para 5.85 onwards.

Effects of a decision

4.77 A public body should take account of the effects of its decision, and where its decision affects a particular person or persons, take account of the affected person's views on the matter.[76]

Policy or guidance

4.78 Where policy or guidance exists which relates to the decision in question, that policy or guidance is likely to be a relevant consideration.[77] Sometimes, legislation will expressly require a public body to take account of guidance.[78] Public bodies should therefore ensure they are aware of, and take into account, any relevant guidance.

Previous decisions

4.79 A public body may be required to take into account a previous decision in a materially similar case. This applies, for example, in relation to decisions on planning appeals.[79]

75 Equality Act 2010 s149.

76 See eg *R (Plantagenet Alliance Ltd) v Secretary of State for Justice* [2014] EWHC 1662 (Admin) at [100], approving *R (Khatun) v Newham LBC* [2004] EWCA Civ 55 at [27].

77 See eg *R (Winder) v Sandwell MBC (Equality and Human Rights Commission intervening)* [2014] EWHC 2617 (Admin).

78 See eg Care Act 2014 s78.

79 *DLA Delivery Ltd v Baroness Cumberlege of Newick* [2018] EWCA Civ 1305 at [29].

Financial considerations

4.80 The extent to which a public body is required or permitted to have regard to financial considerations varies considerably depending on the context. For example, in some areas, financial resources are an irrelevant consideration, such as when deciding what amounts to suitable education for a child,[80] in deciding whether a person was 'in need' of community care services,[81] or in deciding under the Children Act 1989 whether to give assistance to relevant children 'to the extent that his welfare and his educational needs require it'.[82]

4.81 In other areas, a public body is required to have regard to the public cost of its actions when deciding whether to exercise a discretionary power to achieve a public objective.[83] Very many decisions in the education and social care context will include a requirement to take into account financial considerations – for example, deciding how to discharge the duty to meet an adult's eligible needs for care and support,[84] or determining which school should be named in a child's education, health and care plan.[85]

Political considerations

4.82 In some situations, political views are an irrelevant consideration which must not be taken into account. For example, political views were held to be an irrelevant consideration in relation to a decision whether to appoint a committee to investigate a milk marketing scheme,[86] and in relation to the fixing of a sentence of imprisonment.[87] In some contexts, political considerations (such as hoping that a policy will be politically popular) may be taken into account, so long as the power is not used purely to promote electoral advantage, and all relevant considerations are taken into account.[88]

80 *R v East Sussex CC ex p Tandy* [1998] AC 714, HL at 748.

81 *R v Bristol City Council ex p Penfold* (1997–98) 1 CCLR 315, QBD at 322–325.

82 *R (Kebede) v Newcastle City Council* [2013] EWCA Civ 960.

83 *R (Health and Safety Executive) v Wolverhampton City Council* [2012] UKSC 34 at [24]–[25] and [48].

84 Under Care Act 2014 s18.

85 See Children and Families Act 2014 s39(4)(b)(ii), providing that a local authority can refuse to name the school requested by the child's parents if the child attending the school would be 'incompatible with . . . the efficient use of resources'.

86 *Padfield v Minister of Agriculture, Fisheries and Food* [1968] AC 997, HL at 1058, 1061.

87 *R v Secretary of State for the Home Department ex p Venables* [1998] AC 407, HL.

88 *Porter v Magill* [2001] UKHL 67.

Legitimate expectations

4.83 A public body must take account of any legitimate expectations that have arisen in relation to a decision.[89] See further para 4.93 onwards below on the principle of legitimate expectations.

International treaties

4.84 Generally, public bodies are permitted to take into account international treaties as a permissible consideration, but are not required to take them into account.[90] This is related to the principle that international treaties are not part of UK law and do not give rise to legal rights or obligations in domestic law.[91]

ECHR rights

4.85 Public bodies are required to make decisions that are compatible with people's rights under the ECHR.[92] Whilst the courts have sometimes described ECHR rights as 'relevant considerations', under the Human Rights Act 1998 it is necessary to ask instead whether a public body has acted in a way that is compatible with the ECHR. See further chapter 6 on complying with the Human Rights Act 1998.

Related principles

4.86 The issue of relevant and irrelevant considerations often overlaps with, or arises at the same time as, the issue of improper purposes, which is considered at para 4.34 above. When a public body makes a decision for an improper purpose, it is likely that it took into account an irrelevant consideration related to the improper purpose. It can be difficult to distinguish between the two doctrines. It may be easier to win a challenge to a decision based on irrelevant considerations, because it is not necessary to show that the irrelevant consideration was the dominant reason for the decision. This is less stringent than the test for improper purposes.

89 *R (Lumba) v Secretary of State for the Home Department* [2011] UKSC 12.

90 See eg *R (Friends of the Earth Ltd) v Heathrow Airport Ltd* [2020] UKSC 52 in relation to the Paris Agreement.

91 *R (Miller) v Secretary of State for Exiting the European Union* [2017] UKSC 5 at [55].

92 Human Rights Act 1998 s6.

4.87 Another principle related to the issue of relevant and irrelevant considerations is the duty for a decision-maker to carry out a sufficient inquiry prior to making its decision, which means taking reasonable steps to inform itself of all relevant considerations.[93] The court will intervene only if no reasonable authority could have been satisfied, on the basis of the inquiries made, that it possessed the information necessary for its decision.[94]

Consistency

4.88 Decision-makers should act in a broadly consistent way, which usually involves treating like cases alike and different cases differently.

4.89 This has sometimes been expressed as a principle of 'equal treatment'. Until recently, equal treatment was often thought to be a stand-alone requirement for a lawful decision, requiring decision-makers to treat persons equally unless there was a valid reason for treating them differently.

4.90 In fact, there is no stand-alone principle in domestic law[95] of consistency or equal treatment.[96] If a decision-maker is said to have treated two individuals differently when they should have treated them equally, the decision is not unlawful because it goes against a requirement of equal treatment or consistency, or because it seems conspicuously unfair.

4.91 Importantly, however, inconsistent decisions can be unlawful for failure to comply with other principles. The rationality requirement is often relevant here, see para 4.49 above. In order for it to be lawful for a decision-maker to treat two individuals in the same situation differently, or to treat people in different situations the same, there must be a rational basis for this.

4.92 Another potentially relevant principle is 'legitimate expectation', explained at para 4.93 onwards below. Broadly, if a decision-maker gives an individual a legitimate expectation that they will be treated the same as someone in a similar situation, or differently to someone

93 *Secretary of State for Education and Science v Tameside MBC* [1977] AC 1014, HL at 1065.

94 *R (FDA) v Minister for the Cabinet Office* [2018] EWHC 2746 (Admin) at [93]–[94]; *R (Plantagenet Alliance Ltd) v Secretary of State for Justice* [2014] EWHC 1662 (Admin).

95 The position is different, eg, under European Union law.

96 *R (Gallaher Group Ltd) v Competition and Markets Authority* [2018] UKSC 25.

in a different situation, it will be unlawful to act otherwise if doing so would result in unfairness.

Legitimate expectation (or, can a decision-maker change their mind?)

4.93 The principle of legitimate expectation is that, in some circumstances, a public body will be held to its promises, where to break those promises would be unfair.

4.94 It is long established that a person can expect that the existing policy of a public body will be applied to them.[97] Legitimate expectation builds upon this, and applies to the decisions of public bodies to *change* policies or practices. Where a public authority has, by a promise or a practice, created a legitimate expectation that it will act in a certain way, it may not act in a different way if to do so would be so unfair as to amount to an abuse of power.

4.95 A legitimate expectation can be either *procedural* – relating to the need to consult people before making decisions that affect them – or *substantive* – relating to the substance of the decision. It remains controversial as to the extent to which there is a different approach to procedural and substantive legitimate expectations.

4.96 The key questions when considering whether a person has a legitimate expectation that has been breached are:

(1) Does the person in question have a legitimate expectation?
(2) If so, what is it?
(3) Has the public authority frustrated the legitimate expectation, ie broken its promise?
(4) If the promise was substantive rather than procedural, was the breaking of the promise so unfair as to amount to an abuse of power?
(5) If a substantive or procedural legitimate expectation has been frustrated, what remedy should the court award?

What gives a person a legitimate expectation?

4.97 Generally speaking, a legitimate expectation can only be brought about by:

- a promise (whether express or implied); or
- a regular practice (which can be seen as a kind of implied promise).

97 See *Re Findlay* [1985] AC 318, HL at 338.

4.98 Whether or not a promise or a practice gives rise to a legitimate expectation will depend on the particular circumstances.[98] The presence of the following features will make a legitimate expectation more likely:

(1) an assurance which is clear, unambiguous and unqualified;[99]
(2) a regular and consistent practice;
(3) an assurance which is directed at (or at least applies to) the person in question;
(4) an assurance must be made by the same public body against whom it is now enforced;
(5) a promise made publicly rather than privately;
(6) it being reasonable for the individual to rely on the assurance, although reliance has not always been held to be a requirement (see further below);
(7) as a general rule, the individual seeking a promised benefit that is itself lawful;
(8) the individual in question providing all relevant information to the public body; and
(9) 'detrimental reliance' meaning the person has relied upon what was promised by taking certain steps and if the promise were now broken the person would suffer some disadvantage as a result. Some cases have suggested that it is necessary in order for there to be a legitimate expectation for a person to have relied to their detriment upon the assurance given,[100] but others have reached the opposite conclusion[101] since it is considered to be unfair to allow public bodies to break promises just because the people to whom the promises were made cannot prove that they have been disadvantaged.

What kinds of legitimate expectation are there?

4.99 The law currently recognises two categories of legitimate expectation – procedural and substantive.[102] However, the court may not always

98 *R v Inland Revenue Commissioners ex p MFK Underwriting Agents Ltd* [1990] 1 WLR 1545, QBD at 1569.

99 *R (Bancoult) v Secretary of State for Foreign and Commonwealth Affairs* [2008] UKHL 61 at [60].

100 For example, *United Policyholders Group v Attorney General of Trinidad and Tobago* [2016] UKPC 17 at [121].

101 *Re Finucane's Application for Judicial Review* [2019] UKSC 7 at [72].

102 See eg *R v North and East Devon HA ex p Coughlan* [2001] QB 213, CA at [57].

be clear about which category a case falls within,[103] and the usefulness of the distinction has been questioned.[104] Nevertheless, it is helpful to understand the types of situation in which the courts may intervene.

Procedural legitimate expectation

Type 1

> If a public body has given a distinct promise (or has shown by a clear practice) that it will not change a policy or remove a substantive benefit without consulting those affected, then ordinarily it must consult.

4.100 This is often thought of as the classic case of a legitimate expectation. Its effect is that a court will not allow the public authority to bring about the proposed change without first consulting those with the legitimate expectation. Further, there may be a legitimate expectation that a consultation be carried out in a particular way or on a particular basis.[105]

Type 2

> Even in the absence of a distinct promise or clear practice, if a public authority has a policy which distinctly and substantially affects an individual or group who is reasonably relying upon the policy continuing, then ordinarily the authority must consult before bringing about a change to that policy.

4.101 This kind of procedural legitimate expectation is much rarer. In order to arise, the impact of the public body's past policy on potentially affected persons must be 'pressing and focussed'.[106] Those affected persons must have substantial grounds to expect that the substance of the relevant policy would continue for a reasonable

103 See eg *Re Finucane's Application for Judicial Review* [2019] UKSC 7 at [72].

104 See eg *Nadarajah v Secretary of State for the Home Department* [2005] EWCA Civ 1363 at [69].

105 *R (Royal Brompton and Harefield NHS Foundation Trust) v Joint Committee of Primary Care Trusts* [2012] EWCA Civ 472.

106 *R v North and East Devon HA ex p Coughlan* [2001] QB 213, CA at [49].

period.[107] There is conflicting case-law on the issue of what standard of scrutiny the court will apply – it is not entirely clear whether the court will ask whether the decision to change policy without consulting was rational,[108] or whether it will decide for itself, asking whether the change without consultation was fair.[109]

Substantive legitimate expectation

> If a public body has given a distinct promise that it will not change a policy or remove a substantive benefit for a particular person or group, then ordinarily it must keep its promise.

4.102 Whilst now established, this is still the most controversial category. It remains rare for the courts to uphold legitimate expectations of this type. The promise in question will be examined by asking whether 'on a fair reading of the promise it would have been reasonably understood to those to whom it was made'.[110] In principle, the promise may arise from a general policy as well as from an individual assurance. However, in practice it is more likely that a legitimate expectation of this type will be confined to just one person or to a few people, where the promise will be more like a contract with them. In one celebrated case, an individual who had been told that a property providing facilities for the severely disabled would be a permanent home for her, succeeded in her challenge that that promise had been breached by the decision to close the property.[111]

Is the frustration of a substantive legitimate expectation unfair?

4.103 Where a legitimate expectation exists, the public body must take that legitimate expectation into account when it is deciding whether to change its policy or remove a benefit. This means it will always be

107 An example of such a legitimate expectation is where the Inland Revenue had, for over 20 years, accepted late submissions of trading losses from a company for the purposes of obtaining tax relief, but then ended the practice without giving notice to a company affected: *R v Inland Revenue Commissioners ex p Unilever plc* [1996] STC 681, CA.

108 *R (Cheshire East BC) v Secretary of State for the Environment* [2011] EWHC 1975 (Admin) at [82] per Langstaff J.

109 *R (Medway Council) v Secretary of State for Transport, Local Government and the Regions* [2002] EWHC 2516 (Admin) at [32].

110 *Paponette v Attorney General of Trinidad and Tobago* [2010] UKPC 32.

111 *R v North and East Devon HA ex p Coughlan* [2001] QB 213, CA at [30].

unlawful to depart from a policy without taking into account the impact of the change on those individuals and groups affected.[112]

4.104 However, it is not always unlawful for a public body to frustrate a substantive legitimate expectation.[113] The court will balance the interests in upholding the expectation against the public policy interest in frustrating it.[114] This will determine whether or not the decision to frustrate the expectation was lawful. One way of describing the court's task here is that the court must decide whether removing the substantive benefit is so unfair as to amount to an 'abuse of power'.[115]

4.105 If a legitimate expectation case is considered by a court, the court will decide for itself whether the public body's conduct is unfair and amounts to an abuse of power.[116] It will do this by weighing up, on the one hand, the impact of the broken promise upon the affected individual(s) against, on the other, the public interest in the change of policy. If there is a sufficiently strong public interest in a change of policy then this may be stronger than the legitimate expectation, and may 'override' it.[117]

4.106 The following considerations will be important in assessing whether there has been an abuse of power:

- the strength of the countervailing public interest;
- the importance of the benefit to individual(s) affected;
- the number of people affected;
- the nature of the promise;
- whether there is detrimental reliance; and
- the possibility of alternative compensation.

Giving reasons for your decision

4.107 There is still (just) no general obligation on decision-makers to give reasons for their decisions. However, the courts have found that the

112 *R (Bibi) v Newham LBC (No 1)* [2001] EWCA Civ 607 at [39] and [51].

113 Some cases suggest that the test of 'fairness' should also be applied in cases concerning procedural legitimate expectations, eg *R v North and East Devon HA ex p Coughlan* [2001] QB 213, CA at [57].

114 *R v North and East Devon HA ex p Coughlan* [2001] QB 213, CA.

115 *R (Niazi) v Secretary of State for the Home Department* [2008] EWCA Civ 755 at [50].

116 It is not limited to *Wednesbury* review: *R (Bhatt Murphy (a firm)) v Independent Assessor* [2008] EWCA Civ 755 at [28].

117 *R v North and East Devon HA ex p Coughlan* [2001] QB 213, CA.

giving of reasons is required in an increasing number of cases, such that it is now more likely than not that reasons will be required in any given case. In those cases, a decision-maker who fails to give reasons, or who gives only inadequate reasons, will have acted unlawfully and may be required to re-take the decision and give proper reasons for it.

4.108 Decision-makers should therefore always carefully consider whether they are under an obligation to give reasons and, if so, how detailed those reasons need to be. Decision-makers may also wish to consider giving reasons even if they are not legally required to do so. This is because giving reasons promotes lawful decision-making, as well as principles of good administration such as accountability and transparency.

When does the duty to give reasons arise?

4.109 As noted above, there is no general duty to give reasons for administrative decisions.[118] However, legislation requires reasons to be given for a wide range of specific types of decision. The common law also obliges decision-makers to give reasons in many cases.

Duty to give reasons imposed by statute

4.110 Both primary and secondary legislation may require reasons to be given. In many cases, the legislation will *expressly* state that reasons must be given for particular decisions.

4.111 Alternatively, legislation may contain an *implied* duty to give reasons, even if it does not expressly say that reasons are required.[119]

Reasons required under the common law

4.112 The common law requires administrative decision-makers to give reasons for their decision where it would be unfair not to do so. It is not easy to identify the precise circumstances in which procedural fairness requires reasons to be given. The courts have resisted invitations to lay down hard and fast rules as to when reasons will be required, preferring to consider each case on its facts.

118 This long-standing rule of law is regularly confirmed by the courts: see eg *Oakley v South Cambridgeshire DC* [2017] EWCA Civ 71 at [29]; approved by the Supreme Court in *R (Campaign to Protect Rural England, Kent) v Dover DC* [2017] UKSC 79 at [52]–[54].

119 A possibility recognised in *Stefan v General Medical Council* [1999] 1 WLR 1293, PC (UK) at 1297.

4.113 This means that whether or not reasons are required will depend on the particular circumstances of the case. Relevant factors include the nature of the decision-making process; the importance of the decision to the affected person; whether reasons are required in order to identify any error in the decision; and whether there is a strong public interest in the decision.

4.114 However, it is clear that the courts are increasingly willing to find that fairness requires decision-makers to give reasons for their decisions. Public bodies should generally expect to be required to justify a failure to give reasons if their decisions are challenged in court.[120]

4.115 A duty to give reasons also arises when a decision-maker decides to depart from its published policy in a particular case, or not to act in accordance with a person's legitimate expectation.[121] In addition, the courts will be more likely to overturn a decision where they are not presented with any reasoning whatsoever in support of the decision. In such a case, the court may conclude that the decision-maker's real reasons were bad in law, or irrational.[122]

Why is it important to give reasons?

4.116 Giving reasons for a decision is important in many ways.[123] Most significantly, the process of setting out the reasons for a decision helps to ensure that the decision is lawful. It requires the decision-maker to focus on the precise criteria which they are applying, and explain whether those criteria are met or not on the facts of the case before them. It can also help to ensure that the key legal and factual issues are systematically addressed.

4.117 Public bodies that give reasons are less likely to make arbitrary or illogical decisions. In part, this is because the process of giving reasons generally improves the quality of decision-making in the way described above. However, the knowledge that their reasons will be scrutinised by the recipient – and possibly the court – also creates a strong incentive for decision-makers to act rationally and fairly.

120 *Oakley v South Cambridgeshire DC* [2017] EWCA Civ 71 at [30].

121 *EC Gransden & Co Ltd v Secretary of State for the Environment* (1987) 54 P & CR 86, QBD; *R (Bibi) v Newham LBC (No 1)* [2001] EWCA Civ 607.

122 *Padfield v Minister of Agriculture, Fisheries and Food* [1968] AC 997, HL; *R v Civil Service Appeal Board ex p Cunningham* [1992] ICR 816, CA at 824.

123 For a summary of the advantages of giving reasons, see *Oakley v South Cambridgeshire DC* [2017] EWCA Civ 71 at [26] and *R v Higher Education Funding Council ex p Institute of Dental Surgery* [1994] 1 WLR 242, DC at 256–257.

4.118 Reasons are also very important from the perspective of the person who is affected by the decision. The very act of giving reasons is an acknowledgement of the individual's basic interest in knowing how important decisions affecting their life have been made.

4.119 In addition, the provision of reasons will help the affected person to assess whether it is necessary or appropriate to challenge the decision. In order to understand whether the decision-maker has been mistaken as to the correct facts or law, or committed an error of logic, it is often essential to know why a particular decision has been reached.

4.120 Giving reasons may also reduce the likelihood that a decision will be challenged. For example:

- If the person affected by the decision understands why it has been reached, they may be more likely to accept it. This is particularly so where the reasons demonstrate that the decision-maker has carefully considered the applicable law, the particular facts of the case and any arguments put forward by the affected individual.
- Giving reasons may increase public confidence in the decision. This is especially the case where there has been a degree of public participation in the decision-making process. For example, planning decisions are often preceded by a public consultation in which large numbers of people may put forward their views. If the relevant authority decides to grant planning permission without giving any reasons, this may lead to a sense of grievance amongst people opposed to the grant, who could feel that their views have not been properly considered.
- Giving reasons may also increase the legitimacy of a decision, by promoting transparency and accountability in public decision-making.[124]

4.121 A reasoned decision can be informative about a decision-maker's likely approach to similar decisions in future. This can deter poor quality applications, which are likely to fail and therefore waste the time of all concerned.

4.122 The reasons for a decision are also likely to be highly significant should that decision ever be challenged in court. They will help the court to scrutinise the decision and check whether the decision-maker had fallen into error.

124 *R (Campaign to Protect Rural England, Kent) v Dover DC* [2017] UKSC 79 at [55].

What does giving reasons involve?

4.123 The stated reasons should give an adequate explanation of the ultimate decision.[125] The nature and detail of the reasons which are required to give such an explanation will vary from case to case, depending on all the relevant circumstances. For example, the more complex or important a decision is, the more detailed reasoning may be required to explain it.

4.124 The extent of the reasons required may also depend on the intended audience. Reasons that are likely to be read by members of the public with little or no knowledge of the issues will require more by way of background explanation. By contrast, a decision which is addressed to people who are already very familiar with the issues can be more concisely expressed. Where there is a statutory duty to give reasons, the legislation may provide for the reasons to be given in a particular way, or to address certain key issues.

4.125 When assessing whether a written statement of reasons is adequate and intelligible, decision-makers may find it useful to ask the following questions:[126]

- Are the reasons intelligible and comprehensible? Do they make sense as a matter of language and logic?
- Do the reasons set out the main factual and legal issues which arise in the specific case? Can the reader understand the conclusions on those issues, and why they were reached?
- Do the stated reasons address any arguments put forward by the people to whom the decision is addressed? Do they explain why one argument was accepted and another rejected?
- Overall, can the reader understand why the ultimate decision was reached?
- Are the reasons sufficient to enable the affected individuals to assess whether to challenge the decision?

4.126 As long as they are adequate and intelligible, the reasons given for a decision do not have to be perfect, or deal with every single relevant issue. The courts are well aware of the need to avoid imposing too heavy a burden on public authorities and the risks of making the administrative decision-making process too legalistic.

4.127 Decision letters should therefore be read in a straightforward manner, in recognition of the fact that they are often not drafted by

125 *R (Campaign to Protect Rural England, Kent) v Dover DC* [2017] UKSC 79 at [41].

126 Based on Lord Brown's classic statement of the content of the duty to give reasons in *South Buckinghamshire DC v Porter (No 2)* [2004] UKHL 33 at [36].

lawyers.[127] A person who seeks to challenge a decision on the basis of a failure to give reasons will generally have to show that they have suffered some genuine and substantial prejudice as a result.[128]

4.128 However, administrative decision-makers should not assume that they will always be given the opportunity to change or supplement their reasons for a decision should the matter go to court.[129] The courts generally do not allow decision-makers to reconstruct the reasons for their decisions with the benefit of hindsight. The safest approach is therefore for the decision-maker to consider carefully the reasons for their decision at the time, and set them out clearly in accordance with the principles above.

Remedy

4.129 A breach of the duty to give reasons will generally result in the decision in question being quashed.[130] For remedies more generally, see chapter 7.

127 See eg *South Buckinghamshire DC v Porter (No 2)* [2004] UKHL 33 at [36] and *R (Campaign to Protect Rural England, Kent) v Dover DC* [2017] UKSC 79 at [36]–[37] (planning permission); *Holmes-Moorhouse v Richmond upon Thames LBC* [2009] UKHL 7 at [47] (homelessness review decisions).

128 *South Buckinghamshire DC v Porter (No 2)* [2004] UKHL 33 at [36].

129 For example, where there is a statutory duty to give reasons for the decision, the courts will only accept subsequent evidence of the reasons for the decision in exceptional circumstances; in other cases, the courts will be very cautious about accepting 'late' reasons, particularly where they contradict the reasons originally given. See here *R (Nash) v Chelsea College of Art and Design* [2001] EWHC 538 (Admin) at [34]–[35]; *R v Westminster City Council ex p Ermakov* [1996] 2 All ER 302, CA.

130 See eg *R v City of London Corp ex p Matson* [1997] 1 WLR 765, CA.

CHAPTER 5

Complying with the Equality Act 2010

continued

5.1 This chapter seeks to identify the key elements of non-discrimination law under the Equality Act (EA) 2010 and guide decision-makers as to how to ensure compliance with them.[1]

Introduction

5.2 It is fundamental that decision-makers in both the public and private sectors must avoid unlawful discrimination. That principle is easily stated; what is more difficult is to identify precisely what amounts to 'unlawful discrimination', particularly in relation to the more 'subtle' forms of discrimination – for example, an ostensibly neutral policy as to school uniform which puts Black pupils at a disadvantage because of the strictures as to hairstyle, or a transport provider which fails to make reasonable adjustments to cater for the needs of disabled passengers.

5.3 The basic scheme of the EA 2010 is to identify a series of 'protected characteristics', to describe a number of forms of 'prohibited conduct' in relation to people with these characteristics, and then to impose duties on a series of different bodies not to engage in these forms of conduct – ie not to discriminate against people with protected characteristics. The scope of the EA 2010 is huge, covering almost every aspect of society, from the provision of services and the exercise of public functions to employment and associations.

5.4 The EA 2010 came into force on 1 October 2020 and, according to the Explanatory Notes, had two main purposes:

1 The development of equality law in the UK has been rather piecemeal, with the principal legislation in relation to discrimination on grounds of race and sex coming into force in the 1960s and 1970s, including the Race Relations Acts 1965, 1968 and 1976, the Equal Pay Act 1970, and the Sex Discrimination Act 1975 – much of which had its origins in European Union law. These statutes introduced the key legal concepts informing the framework of equality law in the UK, including direct and indirect discrimination, victimisation, and incitement. The law against disability discrimination developed later with the enactment of the Disability Discrimination Act 1995. That Act contained the duty to make reasonable adjustments to address the fact that certain policies ('provisions, criteria or practices') or physical features of premises can put a disabled person at a substantial disadvantage as compared with those who are not disabled. The concept of 'less favourable treatment' in the 1995 Act finds its modern form in the prohibition of 'discrimination arising from disability' under section 15 of the EA 2010.

(1) to harmonise discrimination law (and indeed the Act brought together over 116 separate pieces of legislation[2]); and
(2) to strengthen the law to support progress on equality.

5.5 As well as harmonising existing duties, the EA 2010 also strengthened equality law in certain key respects:

(1) creating a new duty on certain public bodies to consider socio-economic disadvantage when making strategic decisions about how to exercise their functions (although notably only part of this duty is in force);
(2) extending the circumstances in which a person is protected against discrimination, harassment or victimisation because of a protected characteristic; and
(3) creating the public sector equality duty (addressed further at para 5.85 onwards below).[3]

5.6 The EA 2010 has over 200 sections and 28 Schedules. This chapter aims to highlight the most important provisions of the Act to assist decision-makers to achieve compliance with it.

5.7 When considering compliance with the EA 2010, it is also extremely useful to have regard to the codes of practice[4] and guidance produced by the Equality and Human Rights Commission (EHRC).[5]

Protected characteristics

5.8 The EA 2010 identifies certain characteristics that are 'protected', which means that it is unlawful to discriminate in relation to them (where provision is made for this in the relevant Part of the Act):[6]

(1) age;
(2) disability;

2 See Equality and Human Rights Commission (EHRC) *An introduction to the Equality Act 2010* (March 2016), available at www.equalityhumanrights.com/equality/equality-act-2010/what-equality-act
3 EA 2010 Explanatory Notes.
4 The EHRC has produced codes of practice on (i) equal pay, (ii) employment, and (iii) services, public functions and associations, which are available on its website.
5 See www.equalityhumanrights.com/en/
6 For example, section 28 provides that it is not unlawful to discriminate against a person under 18 (ie a child) in relation to the provision of goods and services and the exercise of public functions under section 29, because the characteristic of 'age' only applies to persons aged 18 or over. See further para 5.10 below.

(3) gender reassignment;
(4) marriage and civil partnership;
(5) pregnancy and maternity;
(6) race;
(7) religion or belief;
(8) sex; and
(9) sexual orientation.

Age

5.9 Section 5 of the EA 2010 addresses age. It defines a person who has the particular protected characteristic of age as a 'reference to a person of a particular age group',[7] where an 'age group' is 'a reference to a group of persons defined by reference to age, whether by reference to a particular age or to a range of acts'.[8]

5.10 What this means in practice is that an 'age group' can be wide, including 'over fifties' or 'under thirties', but it can also be narrow, for example, 'people in their mid-eighties' or relative, 'older than me' or 'younger than us'.[9] Age groups are normally grounded in chronological age(s) but age-related terms might identify a particular chronological age group. The protected characteristic of age does not, however, apply to those aged less than 18 in respect of goods, facilities and public functions.[10] However, children who consider they have been discriminated against on grounds of their age by a service provider or public body could bring a claim for breach of their human rights, by reference to Article 14 of the European Convention on Human Rights (ECHR) (discussed further at para 6.56 onwards below).

5.11 The age group with which any comparison should be made depends upon the context and circumstances of a particular case.

Disability

5.12 Determining whether a person has a 'disability' can be complex and it might require specialist legal advice, and potentially expert

7 EA 2010 s5(1)(a).
8 EA 2010 s5(2).
9 A Robinson, D Ruebain and S Uppal, eds *Blackstone's Guide to The Equality Act 2010* (OUP, 4th ed, 2021), para 2.05.
10 EA 2010 s28(1)(a). See further EHRC *Services, public functions and associations: Code of Practice* (January 2011) ('EA 2010 Code'), para 2.4; *Blackstone's Guide to The Equality Act 2010*, paras 2.06–2.10.

evidence.[11] However, in many cases there will be no dispute that the relevant person is 'disabled' for the purposes of the EA 2010.

5.13 Under EA 2010 s6, a person has a disability if (a) that person has a physical or mental impairment and (b) the impairment has a substantial and long-term adverse effect on that person's ability to carry out normal day-to-day activities.[12]

5.14 'Physical or mental impairment' includes 'hidden' impairments, such as mental illness or mental health problems, diabetes, and epilepsy.[13] It also includes sensory impairments such as those affecting sight or hearing.[14] An impairment that consists of a severe disfigurement is treated as having a substantial adverse effect on the person's ability to carry out normal day-to-day activities,[15] but that does not include a tattoo or piercing of the body for decorative or other non-medical purposes.[16] There are also certain other conditions which are generally not to be treated as impairments for the purposes of the definition of disability (including a tendency to steal, a tendency to physical or sexual abuse of other persons, and seasonal allergic rhinitis).[17] Note, however, that if a tendency to physical abuse arises from a recognised impairment such as autism, that person may well remain 'disabled' and benefit from the protection of the EA 2010, including in relation to any physically aggressive behaviour they may display.[18]

11 Supplementary provisions can be found in EA 2010 Sch 1 Part 1 and the Equality Act 2010 (Disability) Regulations 2010 SI No 2128, as well as the Equality Act 2010 guidance: Government Equalities Office *Disability: Equality Act 2010 – Guidance on matters to be taken into account in determining questions relating to the definition of disability* (February 2022), available at www.gov.uk/government/publications/equality-act-guidance/disability-equality-act-2010-guidance-on-matters-to-be-taken-into-account-in-determining-questions-relating-to-the-definition-of-disability-html

12 EA 2010 s6(1).

13 EA 2010 Code, para 2.13.

14 EA 2010 Code, para 2.8.

15 EA 2010 Sch 1 para 3.

16 Equality Act 2010 (Disability) Regulations 2010 reg 5. Addictions to alcohol, nicotine or any other substance are not an impairment for the purposes of the Act (except where the addiction was originally the result of the administration of medically prescribed drugs or other medical treatment): Equality Act 2010 (Disability) Regulations 2010 reg 3.

17 Equality Act 2010 (Disability) Regulations 2010 reg 4.

18 See *C and C v Governing Body of a School, Secretary of State for Education (first interested party), National Autistic Society (second interested party) (SEN)* [2018] UKUT 269 (AAC), where the Upper Tribunal held that it was necessary for the regulation in relation to 'tendency to physical abuse' to be limited in this way to avoid a breach of Article 14 ECHR (the human right to non-discrimination).

5.15 The effect on a person's life is 'substantial' if it is more than minor or trivial.[19] 'Long term' means that the impairment has lasted or is likely to last for at least 12 months or for the rest of the affected person's life.[20] If the impairment ceases to have a substantial adverse effect on a person's ability to carry out normal day-to-day activities, if it is likely to recur, then it is to be treated as continuing to have that effect.[21] Where a person is taking measures to treat or correct an impairment (other than spectacles or contact lenses), and, without those measures, the impairment would be likely to have an adverse effect on the person's ability to carry out normal day-to-day activities, it is still to be treated as though it does have such an effect.[22]

5.16 The EA 2010 contains no definition or list of normal day-to-day activities, but the Court of Justice of the European Union has applied a broad test by asking whether the impairment 'hinders the full and effective participation of the person concerned in professional life over a long period of time'.[23] To ascertain whether an impairment has a substantial adverse effect requires a comparison between the way a person carries out an activity with the impairment and the way they would carry out the activity without it.[24]

5.17 Certain medical conditions are deemed disabilities under the EA 2010 from the point of diagnosis, including cancer, HIV infection and multiple sclerosis.[25] If a person is certified blind, severely sight impaired or partially sighted by a consultant ophthalmologist, they are also deemed to have a disability.[26]

5.18 In most circumstances, a person will have the protected characteristic of disability if they have had a disability in the past, even if they no longer have the disability.[27] Non-disabled people are also protected against direct disability discrimination (and sometimes,

19 EA 2010 s212(1).

20 EA 2010 Sch 1 para 2(1).

21 EA 2010 Sch 1 para 2(1).

22 EA 2010 Sch 1 para 5; EA 2010 Code, para 2.12.

23 Case C-13/05 *Chacón Navas v Eurest Colectividades SA* [2006] ECR I-6467, ECJ. The activity need not be done by both sexes to be treated as a normal day-to-day activity: in *Ekpe v Commissioner of Police of the Metropolis* [2001] ICR 1084, EAT the use of hair rollers was held to be a normal day-to-day activity for a woman.

24 See *Blackstone's Guide to The Equality Act 2010*, para 2.29; and see *Paterson v Commissioner of Police of the Metropolis* [2007] IRLR 763, EAT.

25 EA 2010 Sch 1 para 6; EA 2010 Code, para 2.14.

26 Equality Act 2010 (Disability) Regulations 2010 reg 7.

27 Except in relation to transport and improvements to let dwelling houses: EA 2010 s6(4), Part 12 (transport) and s190 (improvements to dwelling houses).

harassment and victimisation) where they are *perceived* to have a disability or are *associated* with a disabled person.[28]

Gender reassignment

5.19 A person has the protected characteristic of gender reassignment if they are proposing to undergo, are undergoing or have undergone a process (or part of a process) for the purpose of reassigning their sex by changing physiological or other attributes of sex.[29] A reference to a transsexual person is a reference to a person who has the protected characteristic of gender reassignment.[30]

5.20 The EA 2010 Code suggests that 'gender reassignment' is given a broad, non-medical definition – it is a personal process: moving away from one's birth sex to the preferred gender.[31] It may include undergoing medical reassignment treatments, but it does not require any medical process or treatment.[32] This definition is particularly important for children, some of whom may be too young to make the decision to reassign their gender, but have begun a personal process of changing their gender identity (including by way of their mode of dress).[33] Although adopted by an employment tribunal in a high profile case,[34] whether the Code is correct in this description of a broad approach to the 'process' of gender reassignment has not yet been determined by the higher courts (decisions of an employment tribunal do not set any binding precedent).

5.21 This characteristic is protected where, as part of the process of reassigning their sex, someone is driven by their gender identity to cross-dress, not where someone chooses to cross-dress for another reason.[35]

5.22 It is important to note that transsexual people should not be routinely asked to produce their gender recognition certificate as evidence of their legal gender, because that is likely to compromise the individual's right to privacy. If, however, proof of a person's legal

28 EA 2010 Code, para 2.7.
29 EA 2010 s7(1).
30 EA 2010 s7(2).
31 EA 2010 Code, paras 2.19–2.21.
32 EA 2010 Code, paras 2.20–2.21.
33 EA 2010 Code, para 2.21.
34 *Taylor v Jaguar Land Rover Ltd* Case No 1304471/2018 [2020] 9 WLUK 200, ET.
35 EA 2010 Code, para 2.24.

gender is required, then the person's (new) birth certificate should be sufficient confirmation.[36]

Marriage and civil partnership

5.23 The protected characteristic of marriage and civil partnership applies to a person if they are married[37] or are a civil partner.[38] Both marriage and civil partnership include a union between a man and a woman or a same-sex couple. The EA 2010 does not therefore protect single people, divorcees, fiancées, cohabitees, widows or widowers.[39]

5.24 To rely on this protected characteristic, the reason for the less favourable treatment must be the fact that an individual is married or in a civil partnership (rather than the fact of a close relationship).[40]

Pregnancy and maternity

5.25 The EA 2010 protects women from discrimination because of their pregnancy or maternity, which includes breastfeeding.[41] It includes a period of 26 weeks beginning with the day on which the woman gives birth (including to a stillborn baby provided that she was pregnant for at least 24 weeks prior to the birth).[42]

Race

5.26 The protected characteristic of race includes (a) colour, (b) nationality, and (c) ethnic or national origins.[43] 'Colour' includes white, black and brown.[44]

5.27 'Nationality' is defined by citizenship (and is distinct from national origins).[45] 'National origins' must have identifiable elements,

36 EA 2010 Code, para 2.27; the Gender Recognition Act 2004 provides that where a person holds a gender recognition certificate they must be treated according to their acquired gender.

37 See the Marriage Act 1949.

38 EA 2010 s8(1); in respect of civil partnerships, see the Civil Partnership Act 2004.

39 *Blackstone's Guide to The Equality Act 2010*, para 2.55.

40 *Hawkins v Atex Group Ltd and others* [2012] ICR 1315, EAT.

41 EA 2010 ss13(6)(a), 17–18.

42 EA 2010 s17(2)–(5). There are further provisions with respect to employment and maternity leave: see section 18.

43 EA 2010 s9(1).

44 *Blackstone's Guide to The Equality Act 2010*, para 2.57.

45 EA 2010 s9(1)(b).

including historic and geographic, which show the existence of previous existence of a nation.[46]

5.28 When considering 'ethnic origins', one must first consider whether a person belongs to an 'ethnic group', which is a separate and distinct community by virtue of certain characteristics.[47] A group is an ethnic group if it has the following features: a long-shared history and cultural traditions of its own.[48] An ethnic group may also have one or more of the following characteristics: a common language, a common literature, a common religion or geographical origin, or a sense of being a minority or an oppressed or dominant group.[49] The courts have confirmed that the following are protected ethnic groups: Sikhs, Jews, Romany Gypsies, Irish Travellers, Scottish Gypsies and Scottish Travellers.[50]

5.29 'Caste discrimination' is not expressly prohibited by the EA 2010, but it has been held that the concept of 'ethnic origins' is sufficiently wide to capture many aspects of caste discrimination.[51]

5.30 A person has this particular protected characteristic if they fall within a particular racial group.[52] For example, a racial group could be 'British' people, because they share national origins.[53] A racial group can be made up of two or more distinct racial groups, for example, 'Black Britons' would encompass those people who are both Black and British citizens.[54] Racial groups can also be defined by exclusion, for instance, those of 'non-British' nationality.[55]

Religion or belief

5.31 'Religion' includes both religion and lack of religion (thus protecting atheism).[56] The meaning of religion within the EA 2010 is broad and is consistent with ECHR Article 9.[57]

46 EA 2010 Code, para 2.36.
47 EA 2010 Code, paras 2.32–2.35.
48 See the (then) House of Lords' decision in *Mandla v Dowell Lee* [1983] 2 AC 548, HL.
49 *Mandla v Dowell Lee* [1983] 2 AC 548, HL.
50 EA 2010 Code, para 2.35.
51 *Chandhok v Tirkey* [2015] IRLR 195, EAT.
52 EA 2010 s9(2).
53 EA 2010 Code, para 2.39; see also EA 2010 s9(3).
54 EA 2010 Code, para 2.41.
55 EA 2010 Code, para 2.42.
56 EA 2010 s10(1).
57 EA 2010 Code, para 2.45.

5.32 'Religion' includes the more commonly recognised religions, such as Baha'i faith, Buddhism, Christianity, Hinduism, Islam, Jainism, Judaism, Rastafarianism, Sikhism and Zoroastrianism.[58] A religion does not need to be mainstream or well known to be protected under the EA 2010 but it must have a clear structure and belief system – it is ultimately for the courts to determine what constitutes a religion.[59]

5.33 'Belief' is defined as 'any religious or philosophical belief' (including a lack of belief). 'Religious belief' goes beyond beliefs about and adherence to a particular religion or its central articles of faith.[60] 'Philosophical belief' includes Humanism and Atheism.[61] To be protected under the EA 2010, a philosophical belief:

- must be genuinely held;
- must be a belief, and not an opinion or viewpoint, based on the present state of information available;
- must be a belief as to a weighty and substantial aspect of human life and behaviour;
- must attain a certain level of cogency, seriousness, cohesion and importance; and
- must be worthy of respect in a democratic society, not incompatible with human dignity and not in conflict with the fundamental rights of others.[62]

5.34 A 'manifestation of religion or beliefs' contrasts with holding a religion or belief. A 'manifestation' of such a belief is when there is a 'sufficiently close and direct nexus between the act and the underlying belief'.[63] Individuals have an absolute right to hold a belief under the ECHR, but the manifestation of that belief is qualified and may need to be limited in certain circumstances.[64] The EA 2010 Code, however, warns that 'there is not always a clear line between holding a religion or belief and the manifestation of that religion or belief' –

58 EA 2010 Code, para 2.46.

59 EA 2010 Code, para 2.47.

60 EA 2010 Code, para 2.49.

61 EA 2010 Code, para 2.50.

62 EA 2010 Code, para 2.52; see also: *Grainger plc and others v Nicholson* [2010] 2 All ER 253, EAT; *McClintock v Department of Constitutional Affairs* [2008] IRLR 29, EAT; *R (Williamson and others) v Secretary of State for Education and Employment and others* [2005] UKHL 15.

63 *Eweida v United Kingdom* (App No 48420/10) [2013] ECHR 37, ECtHR.

64 EA 2010 Code, para 2.53.

thus, placing limitations on a person's right to manifest their religion or belief may constitute a form of unlawful discrimination.[65]

Sex

5.35 Sex refers to a male or a female of any age.[66] As detailed at para 5.25 above, there are specific provisions relating to maternity and pregnancy.

Sexual orientation

5.36 Sexual orientation means a person's sexual orientation towards a person of the same sex, a person of the opposite sex or persons of either sex.[67] Sexual orientation relates to how people feel as well as their actions.[68]

Prohibited conduct

5.37 The EA 2010 defines the specific matters constituting 'prohibited conduct' (unlawful discrimination).[69] For the most part, the prohibited conduct is defined in the same way for each protected characteristic, but there are certain exceptions, particularly for disability. The Act defines specific forms of disability discrimination (including discrimination arising from disability and a duty to make reasonable adjustments, addressed further at para 5.69 below). We outline below some of the main forms of discriminatory conduct prohibited under the EA 2010.

Direct discrimination

5.38 Direct discrimination is probably the most straightforward in terms of prohibited conduct (or at least the one that most obviously comes to mind when discrimination is thought of): it concerns different

65 EA 2010 Code, para 2.54.
66 EA 2010 ss11(a)–(b), 212(1).
67 EA 2010 s12(1).
68 EA 2010 Code, para 2.59.
69 EA 2010 Part 2 Ch 2.

treatment between two individuals where the reason for that difference is the protected characteristic itself.[70]

5.39 There are three components of direct discrimination. These are:

(1) first, the treatment experienced by 'A' must be *different* from that of another person (the 'comparator'), 'B';
(2) second, the treatment of A must be *less favourable* than the treatment of B; and
(3) third, the less favourable treatment must be *because of* a protected characteristic.

5.40 The circumstances of a comparator need not be the same in all respects – it is a question of fact and degree, which means it is case-specific.[71] A comparator can also be a hypothetical person, but that can prove challenging.[72] In some cases, the fact that someone cannot be a comparator because their situation is materially different from that of the claimant might also provide an indication of how a hypothetical comparator is likely to have been treated in the claimant's circumstances. The rejection of an actual comparator might also help a decision-maker to assess what an appropriate hypothetical comparator might be.

5.41 There is a low threshold for treatment to be less favourable. A must be subject to some disadvantage – it need not only be a tangible or material loss.[73] It can include being deprived of a choice or excluded from an opportunity.[74] It need only be enough to give the claimant a 'justified sense of grievance'. The EA 2010 Code explains that it is enough for an individual to 'reasonably say that they would have preferred not to be treated differently from the way the service provider treated – or would have treated – another person'.[75] The EA 2010 also specifically states that racial segregation constitutes less favourable treatment.[76] In such circumstances, there is no need to identify a comparator, because racial segregation is always discriminatory, but

70 EA 2010 s13(1).

71 See *Hewage v Grumpian Health Board* [2012] UKSC 37 at [21]–[23] for a discussion of the types and differences that may affect compatibility.

72 See *Shamoon v Chief Constable of the Royal Ulster Constabulary* [2003] UKHL 11.

73 *Chief Constable of West Yorkshire v Khan* [2001] UKHL 48 at [52]–[53]; *R v Birmingham City Council ex p Equal Opportunities Commission (No 1)* [1989] AC 1155, HL.

74 EA 2010 s31(7) and EA 2010 Code, para 4.5.

75 EA 2010 Code, para 4.6.

76 EA 2010 s13(5).

segregation must be a deliberate act or policy rather than a situation that has occurred inadvertently.[77]

5.42 Finally, whilst the reason for the less favourable treatment needs to be the protected characteristic,[78] it does not need to be the only or even the main cause.[79] An individual's motive in respect of the treatment is irrelevant; and it does not matter whether the less favourable treatment was conscious or unconscious.[80]

Exceptions

5.43 Whilst direct discrimination is generally unlawful, there are certain exceptions, for example:

(1) When a disabled person is treated more favourably than a non-disabled person.[81]
(2) In respect of the protected characteristic of age, the position is more complicated – if it can be shown that the treatment of A compared to the treatment of B was a proportionate means of achieving a legitimate aim, then that can constitute an objective justification. The 'legitimate aim' must fall into one of two main categories: inter-generational fairness and dignity.[82]
(3) The components of direct discrimination in respect of pregnancy and maternity is slightly different – the test is unfavourable treatment rather than less favourable; and therefore there is no need for a comparator.[83] The unfavourable treatment (which means that she is put at a disadvantage) will be pregnancy or maternity discrimination if a woman would not have received the treatment but for the fact that she is or has been pregnant, has given birth within the previous 26 weeks or is breastfeeding a baby that is more than 26 weeks old.[84]

77 EA 2010 Code, para 4.9.

78 *R (E) v Governing Body of JFS and the Admission Appeals Panel of JFS others* [2009] UKSC 15 at [13]; *R v Birmingham City Council ex p Equal Opportunities Commission (No 1)* [1989] AC 1155, HL; *James v Eastleigh BC* [1990] 2 AC 751, HL.

79 EA 2010 Code, para 4.12.

80 EA 2010 Code, para 4.15; *Nagarajan v London Regional Transport* [2000] 1 AC 501, HL and *Amnesty International v Ahmed* [2009] IRLR 884, EAT.

81 EA 2010 ss158, 159 and 13(3); EA 2010 Code, para 4.33.

82 *Seldon v Clarkson Wright & Jakes* [2012] UKSC 16.

83 EA 2010 s17.

84 EA 2010 s17; EA 2010 Code, paras 4.34–4.38.

Discrimination based upon perception or association

5.44 The individual experiencing less favourable treatment does not have to possess the protected characteristic themself. There are two further types of direct discrimination:

(1) discrimination by association; and
(2) discrimination by perception.

Neither applies in respect of the protected characteristic of pregnancy or maternity.

5.45 As to discrimination by association, this might occur when A is treated less favourably than B because A is associated with another person who has a protected characteristic.[85] The association with the other person does not need to be permanent. It can also occur where an individual campaigned to help people with a particular protected characteristic or refused to act in a way that would disadvantage a person or people who have the characteristic.[86]

5.46 Discrimination by perception can occur when A treats B less favourably because A mistakenly thinks that B has a protected characteristic.

Indirect discrimination

5.47 Indirect discrimination is more difficult to identify. It applies to all protected characteristics except pregnancy and maternity (although in situations that might otherwise engage pregnancy and maternity, there might instead be indirect sex discrimination).[87]

5.48 Indirect discrimination occurs when an *apparently neutral* provision, criterion or practice (PCP) (the meaning of which is considered further at para 5.49 below) is applied, which puts persons sharing a protected characteristic at a particular disadvantage, and the PCP cannot be justified.[88] There are therefore four components to indirect discrimination:

(1) A applies (or would apply) the PCP equally to everyone within the relevant group including B;

85 EA 2010 Code, para 4.19.
86 EA 2010 Code, para 4.19.
87 EA 2010 Code, para 5.2.
88 EA 2010 s19(1)–(2); *Essop v Home Office UK (Border Agency)* [2017] UKSC 27 at [24].

(2) the PCP puts (or would put) people who share B's protected characteristic at a particular disadvantage when compared with people who do not have that characteristic;
(3) the PCP puts (or would put) B at that disadvantage; and
(4) A cannot show that the PCP is justified as a proportionate means of achieving a legitimate aim.

What is a PCP?

5.49 A PCP should be interpreted broadly to include any formal or informal policies, rules, practices, arrangements, criteria, conditions, prerequisites, qualifications or provisions, as well as a 'one-off' or discretionary decision.[89] It must at least appear neutral, otherwise direct discrimination ought to be considered.

What is a disadvantage?

5.50 A 'disadvantage' includes a denial of an opportunity or choice, deterrence, rejection, or exclusion. It can be used interchangeably with a 'detriment', which is something that a reasonable person would complain about.[90]

Who is put at a disadvantage?

5.51 When thinking about a disadvantage two steps need to be considered:
(1) first, in respect of a *group* of people sharing the individual's protected characteristic, the PCP puts or *would* put that group at a particular disadvantage; *and*
(2) second, the PCP puts or *would* put the particular individual at that disadvantage.

5.52 Once a link has been established between the protected characteristic and the disadvantage that it causes, then a comparison is required as between the impact of the PCP on those individuals who have the protected characteristic and those that do not.[91] Further, there must be no material difference between the circumstances

89 EA 2010 Code, paras 5.6–5.7.
90 EA 2010 Code, para 5.10.
91 EA 2010 s19(2)(b)–(c).

relating to each case.[92] In undertaking the comparison, the following questions should be adopted:[93]

(1) What proportion of the pool has the particular protected characteristic?
(2) Within the pool, does the PCP affect individuals without the protected characteristic?
(3) How many of those individuals are (or would be) disadvantaged by it? How is this expressed as a proportion ('X')?
(4) Within the pool, how does the PCP affect individuals who share the protected characteristic?
(5) How many of those individuals are (or would be) put at a disadvantage by it? How is this expressed as a proportion ('Y')?

5.53 Once it has been established that a PCP puts a group with a particular protected characteristic at a disadvantage, then one needs to prove that the individual bringing the claim is put (or would be put) at that disadvantage.

Objective justification?

5.54 In certain circumstances, an apparently neutral PCP that puts a person with a particular protected characteristic at a disadvantage can be objectively justified and therefore does *not* constitute unlawful indirect discrimination.[94]

5.55 The UK Supreme Court has identified a four-stage approach to assessing the proportionality of a measure or decision:[95]

(1) first, whether the purported legitimate aim is sufficiently important to justify the potentially discriminatory treatment;
(2) second, whether there is any rational connection between this aim and the less favourable treatment or disadvantage suffered;
(3) third, whether the means chosen to meet the aim are no more than is necessary to accomplish it (and whether proportionate

92 EA 2010 s23(1).

93 EA 2010 Code, para 5.21. Sedley LJ observed in *Allonby v Accrington and Rossendale College* [2001] EWCA Civ 529 that the identifying the pool was not a matter of discretion or of fact-finding but of logic (at [19]); he further indicated that there are some guiding principles, including, 'the pool should not be so drawn as to incorporate the disputed condition'. The pool should be chosen such that suitably tests the particular discrimination complained of: see also Sedley LJ in *Grundy v British Airways plc* [2007] EWCA Civ 1020.

94 EA 2010 s19(2)(d).

95 *Akerman-Livingstone v Aster Communities Ltd* [2015] UKSC 15 at [28]–[29] per Lady Hale DPSC.

alternative measures could have been taken without a discriminatory effect); and

(4) fourth, whether the steps complained of strike a fair balance between the need to accomplish the aim and the detriment suffered.

5.56 Legitimate aims must be lawful, and might include:[96]

(1) ensuring that services and benefits are targeted at those who most need them;
(2) the fair exercise of powers;
(3) preventing fraud and other forms of abuse by individuals; and
(4) ensuring the wellbeing or dignity of individuals, for example, using a service.

5.57 Assessing whether the PCP is a proportionate means of achieving an aim essentially involves a balancing exercise as between, on the one hand, the discriminatory effect of a PCP and, on the other, the reasons for applying it (taking into account all the relevant facts).[97] Bearing that in mind, the more serious the disadvantage (and the discriminatory effect), the more convincing the objective justification must be.[98] The fact that a less discriminatory PCP might be more expensive does not mean that the PCP is justified. Cost cannot on its own provide a justification for a particular PCP. However, cost can be taken into account as part of the justification if there are other good reasons for the PCP.[99]

5.58 When a public authority is considering whether it can justify what might otherwise constitute unlawful indirect discrimination, an important factor is the extent to which the authority has complied with its public sector equality duties (discussed more at para 5.85 onwards below).[100]

5.59 The interplay between indirect discrimination in respect of disability and other forms of disability discrimination can be complex. If a neutral PCP puts individuals with a particular disability at a disadvantage then it might be that the PCP does not need to be changed because of a parallel duty, namely the duty to make reasonable adjustments, which means that the PCP will be adjusted for those with that disability.[101]

96 EA 2010 Code, para 5.30.
97 EA 2010 Code, para 5.31.
98 EA 2010 Code, para 5.34.
99 EA 2010 Code, para 5.33.
100 EA 2010 Code, para 5.36.
101 EA 2010 Code, para 5.39.

Discrimination arising from disability

5.60 The EA 2010 prohibits service providers and those carrying out public functions from treating disabled people unfavourably for a reason connected with that individual's disability.[102] It is important to flag that discrimination arising from disability is *different* from direct discrimination because of disability itself, as it concerns unfavourable treatment because of something arising *as a consequence* of someone's disability.[103] As such, it offers far broader protection against unfavourable treatment for disabled people than the prohibition on direct discrimination. However, unlike direct discrimination on grounds of disability, discrimination arising from disability includes a justification defence.

5.61 This prohibited conduct occurs when:[104]

(1) A treats B (a disabled person) unfavourably because of something arising in consequence of B's disability; and
(2) the treatment is not a proportionate means of achieving a legitimate aim.

5.62 If, however, A shows that they did not know, and could not reasonably be expected to know, that B had the disability, this also provides a defence.[105]

What is unfavourable treatment?

5.63 As above, unfavourable treatment means that the individual has been put at a disadvantage – it can include being denied a choice or excluded from an opportunity. When thinking about possible disadvantage, careful consideration needs to be given as to less obvious forms of disadvantage, particularly in circumstances when A thinks that they are acting in the best interests of the disabled person.[106]

What does 'something arising in consequence of disability' mean?

5.64 The consequences of a disability can include anything which is the result, effect or outcome of a disabled person's disability – some are obvious, others require investigation and further consideration (for

102 EA 2010 s15.
103 EA 2010 Code, para 6.4.
104 EA 2010 Code, para 6.4.
105 EA 2010 s15(2).
106 EA 2010 Code, para 6.8; EA 2010 s15(1)(a).

example, as a result of someone's disability, they might not be able to understand the implications of a financial agreement). Typical matters which arise in consequence of a person's disability can include how they behave or how they communicate. As such, if an autistic child strikes a teaching assistant out of frustration at having been made to queue up for their school dinner and is then excluded from school, this may well be said to be a punishment that is given because of something arising in consequence of their disability, ie their behaviour.[107]

When can this conduct be justified?

5.65 This is addressed at para 5.54 onwards above in respect of indirect discrimination – it is the same test of objective justification. It requires evidence in support.

Does A know or should they know about the disability?

5.66 Whether A knows about B's disability is a matter of fact. What is required is knowledge of the facts which, in law, meet the definition of disability, rather than knowledge that the definition of disability is met, or even that there is such a legal definition.

5.67 Whether A should (ie they could reasonably be expected to) know that a person is disabled requires investigation into the relevant circumstances. The extent and scope of that investigation will depend upon what is reasonable in the particular circumstances. Whether A could reasonably be expected to know will be assessed objectively.

5.68 The sorts of considerations that may help to assess this might include:

- The role that the decision-maker fulfils in the circumstances of the case.
- The resources available to or which might be called upon by the decision-maker.
- The nature and extent of public law powers available to or being relied upon by the decision-maker. For example, what is reasonable to expect of a service-provider on a one-off basis is likely to be different from the expectations of a public body such as a local

107 See *C and C v Governing Body of a School, Secretary of State for Education (first interested party), National Autistic Society (second interested party) (SEN)* [2018] UKUT 269 (AAC) for the rule that such a child would not have a 'tendency to physical abuse' and therefore be excluded from the protection of the EA 2010 (although the extent of the physically aggressive behaviour would plainly be relevant on the question of whether the exclusion could be justified).

authority or a school, which might reasonably be expected to take greater (or even greater) care to identify disabled people, not only because of their duties under the EA 2010 but also because of their general public duties, including obligations under the Human Rights Act 1998 (see chapter 6).

- What the claimant did or did not mention about their disability and why.

Reasonable adjustments

5.69 Under the EA 2010, there is also a duty to make reasonable adjustments for disabled people.[108] Failure to make a reasonable adjustment is an act of unlawful discrimination (and would entitle a disabled person to bring a legal claim). However, it is important to keep in mind that the duty to make reasonable adjustments is not 'free standing' but relates to specific matters, typically a PCP (see para 5.49 above).

5.70 This duty requires certain organisations (including public authorities) and individuals to take positive steps to meet the needs of disabled people, which means that these needs must be ***anticipated***.[109] That means that those providing a service or exercising a public function should not wait for a disabled person to try to use their service, but must plan to meet the needs of potential disabled service users.[110] It applies regardless of whether the service provider or those exercising public functions know that a particular person is disabled.[111] It is also a continuing and evolving duty: this means that it should be kept under regular review in light of the experience of disabled people using the service or affected by the exercise of the public function.[112] Following a review, it might be that a step which was originally reasonable is no longer sufficient and further adjustments might be required.[113]

108 See EA 2010 ss20–22 and Sch 2. Note that there is special provision with respect to transport.

109 EA 2010 Code, para 7.3; *University of Bristol v Abrahart* [2024] EWHC 299 (KB).

110 EA 2010 Code, para 7.21.

111 EA 2010 Code, para 7.22.

112 EA 2010 Code, para 7.27.

113 EA 2010 Code, para 7.27.

5.71 There are three specific requirements as part of this duty for those providing services or exercising public functions. They are:[114]

(1) If a particular policy (PCP, as defined at para 5.49 above) puts disabled people at a substantial disadvantage compared with those that are not, then the duty requires that reasonable steps are taken to avoid that disadvantage.
(2) If a physical feature puts disabled people at a substantial disadvantage compared with those who do not have a disability, then the obligation requires that steps are taken to remove that disadvantage or adopt a reasonable alternative method of providing the service or exercising the public function.
(3) To prove an auxiliary aid in circumstances where not providing such an aid would put disabled people at a substantial disadvantage.

5.72 The duty essentially requires that, so far as is reasonably practicable, access for disabled people is the same as that offered to the public at large.

What is meant by substantial disadvantage to engage this duty?

5.73 The disadvantage needs to be more than minor or trivial; this is a low threshold.[115] The disadvantage created by lack of a reasonable adjustment is measured by reference to what the position would be if the disabled person in question did not have a disability.[116]

What is a PCP in the context of this duty?

5.74 A PCP in the context of this duty is the same as detailed at para 5.49 above in the context of indirect discrimination. It might be that a particular PCP puts a disabled person at a substantial disadvantage; in such circumstances, it might be reasonable to change the PCP so that it no longer has that effect, which might include waiving it or making exceptions.[117]

What is an auxiliary aid in the context of this duty?

5.75 An auxiliary aid or service is anything that provides support or assistance to a disabled person, and includes:

(1) a special piece of equipment;

114 EA 2010 s20 and Sch 2.
115 EA 2010 s20(6).
116 EA 2010 Code, para 7.13.
117 EA 2010 Code, para 7.42.

(2) the provision of a sign language interpreter, lip-speaker or deaf-blind communicator;
(3) extra staff assistance to disabled people;
(4) an electronic or manual note-taking service;
(5) an induction loop or infrared broadcast system;
(6) video phones;
(7) audio-visual fire alarms;
(8) readers for people with visual impairments;
(9) assistance with guiding; and
(10) telephone services to supplement other information.[118]

5.76 The duty to provide auxiliary aids or services includes: (1) ensuring that the aids are properly maintained; and (2) ensuring contingency arrangements are in place in case of an unexpected failure of an aid.[119] The duty does not extend to providing an aid for an individual's personal use.[120] It is important to note, as the list above makes clear, that people (for example, an additional teaching assistant) can be an auxiliary aid or service.

What does the duty require with respect to physical features?

5.77 The duty requires that reasonable steps are taken in respect of a substantial disadvantage caused by a physical feature. First, a 'physical feature' is very broadly defined, and can include features that are temporary (as well as permanent), and fixtures, fittings, furniture and equipment.[121] Second, reasonable steps might require removing the physical feature, altering it or providing a reasonable means of avoiding it.[122] If the substantial disadvantage cannot be avoided by these steps, then thought will need to be given to whether there is a reasonable alternative method of making the service available. What will make the alternative method 'reasonable' will involve consideration

118 EA 2010 Code, para 7.47.
119 EA 2010 Code, para 7.46.
120 EA 2010 Code, para 7.49.
121 EA 2010 Code, para 7.60; the EA 2010 Code provides the following further examples of physical features (para 7.61): steps, stairways, kerbs, exterior surfaces and paving, parking areas, building entrances and exits (including emergency escape routes), internal and external doors, gates, toilet and washing facilities, public facilities (such as telephones, counters or service desks), lighting and ventilation, lifts and escalators, floor coverings, signs, furniture, and temporary or movable items (such as equipment and display racks). Physical features also include the sheer scale of premises (eg the size of a shopping centre).
122 EA 2010 s20(9), Sch 2 paras 1–2, Sch 15 paras 1–2(3), 2(5)–(8).

of whether it significantly offends the dignity of disabled people and the extent to which it causes inconvenience to the disabled person.[123]

What is a 'reasonable' step?

5.78 The duty requires that reasonable steps are taken in order to make adjustments. What is 'reasonable' depends upon all the circumstances of the case, and will vary according to:[124]

(1) the type of service being provided;
(2) the nature of the service provider and its size and resources; and
(3) the effect of the disability on the individual disabled person.

5.79 Some factors that might be relevant depending upon the case include:[125]

(1) Would the particular steps be effective in overcoming the substantial disadvantage faced by disabled people?
(2) To what extent is it practicable to take the steps in question?
(3) What are the financial and other costs of making the adjustment?
(4) What is the likely extent of any disruption caused by taking the step?
(5) How much has already been spent on making adjustments?

5.80 As the EA 2010 Code acknowledges, there are 'no hard and fast solutions' in respect of reasonable adjustments.[126] It is, however, important to note that what is 'reasonable' is ultimately an objective question – it is not therefore sufficient to indicate that you personally (or as an organisation) considered that the adjustment was reasonable. If there is a reasonable adjustment that can be put in place to remove or reduce the substantial disadvantage, it is not sufficient for the service provider to take a lesser step.[127] Indeed, when considering a possible reasonable adjustment, it is important to ascertain whether it will actually and in practice remove or reduce the substantial disadvantage.

What are the limits of this duty?

5.81 It is important to note that a failure to make reasonable adjustments cannot be justified (which contrasts with, for example, indirect discrimination). There are, however, certain limits on the duty insofar as relevant to public authorities and service providers:

123 EA 2010 Code, para 7.57.
124 EA 2010 Code, para 7.29.
125 EA 2010 Code, para 7.30.
126 EA 2010 Code, para 7.34.
127 EA 2010 Code, para 7.35.

(1) first, those exercising public functions are not required to take any steps that are outside their powers;[128]
(2) second, the service provider will not be required to take any steps that would fundamentally alter the nature of the service;[129] and
(3) third, it is not expected that the needs of every individual are anticipated, but the duty requires that consideration is given, and reasonable steps are taken, to overcome barriers that may impede people with different kinds of disability.[130]

Cost of the reasonable adjustment

5.82 The cost of the adjustment (and so the cost of complying with the duty) cannot be passed on to the disabled person, unless expressly permitted.[131] However, the cost of making the adjustment will be relevant to the prior question of whether it is reasonable to make it. Once this has been established, the adjustment must (generally) be made free of charge.

Pregnancy and maternity discrimination

5.83 Discrimination because of pregnancy and maternity includes:[132]

(1) A discriminating against B (a woman) if A treats her *unfavourably* (rather than less favourably) because of her pregnancy; and
(2) A discriminating against B (a women) if, in the period of 26 weeks beginning with the day on which she gives birth, A treats her unfavourably because she has given birth (including because she is breastfeeding).

Harassment

5.84 The EA 2010 prohibits three different types of harassment:[133]

(1) harassment related to a relevant protected characteristic (which are age, disability, gender reassignment, race, religion or belief, sex and sexual orientation);

128 EA 2010 Sch 2 para 2(8).
129 EA 2010 Sch 2 para 2(7).
130 EA 2010 Code, para 7.54.
131 *Blackstone's Guide to The Equality Act 2010*, para 3.65.
132 EA 2010 s17, which relates to pregnancy and maternity discrimination in non-work cases; section 18 addresses pregnancy and maternity discrimination in the context of work cases.
133 EA 2010 s26.

(2) sexual harassment; and
(3) less favourable treatment of an individual because they submit to or reject sexual harassment or harassment related to sex or gender reassignment.

Advancement of equality – public sector equality duty

5.85 The public sector equality duty (PSED) requires that a public authority in the exercise of its functions has *due regard* to a series of specified needs, being the need to:

(a) eliminate discrimination, harassment, victimisation and any other conduct that is prohibited by or under this Act;
(b) advance equality of opportunity between persons who share a relevant protected characteristic and persons who do not share it;
(c) foster good relations between persons who share a relevant protected characteristic and persons who do not share it.[134]

5.86 This duty also applies to those who are not public authorities when they exercise public functions.[135] The duty applies in respect of the following protected characteristics: age, disability, gender reassignment, pregnancy and maternity, race, religion or belief, sex and sexual orientation.[136]

5.87 The concept of 'due regard' is highly sensitive to facts and context. How intense the 'regard' must be to satisfy the requirements in EA 2010 s149 will depend on the circumstances of the decision-making process in which the duty is engaged.[137]

5.88 When considering the need to advance equality of opportunity, public authorities must specifically consider the need to:

(a) remove or minimise disadvantages suffered by persons who share a relevant protected characteristic that are connected to that characteristic;
(b) take steps to meet the needs of persons who share a relevant protected characteristic that are different from the needs of others who do not share it;

134 EA 2010 s149(1).
135 EA 2010 s149(2).
136 EA 2010 s149(7).
137 *R (Sheakh) v Lambeth LBC* [2022] EWCA Civ 457 at [56].

(c) encourage persons who share a relevant protected characteristic to participate in public life or in any other activity in which participation by such persons is disproportionately low.[138]

5.89 Fostering good relations between those who have a protected characteristic and those who do not includes, in particular, the need to tackle prejudice and promote understanding.[139]

5.90 In order to comply with this duty, the following questions will be helpful:

(1) Have the relevant protected characteristics that might be affected by your decision and/or policy and/or exercise of your public function been identified?
(2) Have steps been taken to gather all the relevant information to understand which protected characteristics might be affected and what the impact might be on them?[140]
(3) Once relevant information has been gathered, did it become apparent that anyone else with a protected characteristic might be affected?
(4) Does the relevant information consider the possible impact on the group(s) with the protected characteristic (including the degree and extent of that impact)?[141]
(5) Is there evidence of specific consideration of each of the relevant specified needs listed above in relation to each of the protected characteristics?
(6) Is there evidence that this consideration was taken into account in the decision-making process with an open mind at each stage?[142]

5.91 The courts have repeatedly emphasised that the PSED is a 'process' duty, not a duty to achieve a particular result. The purpose of the PSED has been said to be that 'these considerations of equality of opportunity . . . are now to be placed at the centre of formulation of policy by all public authorities, side by side with all other pressing circumstances of whatever magnitude'.[143]

138 EA 2010 s149(3).

139 EA 2010 s149(5).

140 *R (Hurley and Moore) v Secretary of State for Business, Innovation and Skills* [2012] EWHC 201 (Admin) at [89]–[90].

141 *R (Bailey) v Brent LBC* [2011] EWCA Civ 1586 at [90].

142 *R (Brown) v Secretary of State for Work and Pensions* [2008] EWHC 3158 (Admin) at [90]–[96]; *Hotak v Southwark LBC* [2015] UKSC 30 at [78].

143 *R (Bracking) v Secretary of State for Work and Pensions* [2013] EWCA Civ 1345 at [59].

5.92 It is open to a decision-maker to comply with the PSED by paying 'due regard' to the relevant needs, but nonetheless go on to take a decision which may conflict with them because of other countervailing factors. What matters is that decision-makers 'confront the anticipated consequences in a conscientious and deliberate way in so far as they impact upon the equality objectives'.[144]

5.93 Compliance (or not) with the PSED can be an important factor in assessing the proportionality of a decision that is said to be indirectly discriminatory. That is because a decision that is or appears to be tainted by a failure to give 'due regard' to the PSED ought to be scrutinised more sceptically when a decision-maker seeks to justify the proportionality of a related measure or decision. In general terms, this is consistent with the broad aims of anti-discrimination legislation and the onus placed on public bodies to be proactive in identifying and responding to actual or potentially discriminatory impacts.[145]

5.94 However, some recent decisions in the tribunals[146] and the higher courts[147] indicate that the impact of potential non-compliance with the PSED for the purposes of a proportionality assessment should not be overstated. The relevant legal principles may be more specifically summarised as follows:

(1) In principle, failure to comply with the PSED is a factor to be considered when assessing the proportionality of a particular measure or decision.
(2) However, it remains possible for a decision-maker to justify the proportionality of a measure or decision which is (or might) be tainted by a failure to have due regard to the PSED.
(3) In the absence of any express requirement to the contrary, a decision-maker can provide evidence (or invite reasonable inferences) which demonstrates compliance with the PSED, even after the measure or decision in question has been taken.
(4) It is nonetheless good practice for a decision-maker to keep contemporaneous records demonstrating consideration of the PSED – doing so may prevent an issue becoming the subject of litigation in the first place.

144 *R (Bracking) v Secretary of State for Work and Pensions* [2013] EWCA Civ 1345 at [72].

145 See eg *G v St Gregory's Catholic Science College Governors* [2011] EWHC 1452 (Admin) at [42] per Collins J.

146 See eg *GP v The Lime Trust and Equality and Human Rights Commission* [2023] UKUT 77 (AAC).

147 See eg *R (TZA, anonymity order in place) v A Secondary School* [2023] EWHC 1722 (Admin).

5.95 There is recent Upper Tribunal authority which holds that jurisdictional limitations on certain tribunals might render consideration of arguments about compliance with the PSED 'legally irrelevant'.[148] However, it is submitted that these situations will be relatively rare and, where necessary, ought to be the subject of specific legal advice.

5.96 For completeness, it should be noted that, all else being equal, if a failure to comply with the PSED also demonstrated an issue of direct discrimination, questions of justification would not arise, since direct discrimination cannot be justified.

148 In *GP v The Lime Trust* [2023] UKUT 77 (AAC), Upper Tribunal Judge Wright held that consideration of arguments by the First-tier Tribunal (Special Educational Needs and Disability) had been 'legally irrelevant', even as an adjuct to an argument about the proportionality of a decision to exclude a disabled pupil from his school because the PSED can only be enforced in an application for judicial review, which the First-tier Tribunal had no power to consider. See in particular at [27]–[31], [34]–[43] and [46]–[57].

CHAPTER 6

Complying with the Human Rights Act 1998

6.1 This chapter discusses the requirements on a decision-maker to take decisions which respect the human rights of those subject to them. The focus is on those rights which were incorporated into domestic law by the Human Rights Act (HRA) 1998, being the majority of the rights contained in the European Convention on Human Rights (ECHR, 'Convention'). Some decisions will clearly impact on rights created by other instruments; for example, decisions by schools will often impact on pupils' rights under the UN Convention on the Rights of the Child. While all relevant human rights should be taken into account in decision-making, the ECHR rights have particular importance because parliament has chosen to make them directly enforceable in our courts through the HRA 1998. Many of these rights are closely related to rights found under the common law, which are discussed in chapter 4.

Introduction

6.2 The HRA 1998 incorporated the Convention into our domestic law. The Convention is an international legal treaty, created by the Council of Europe[1] following the Second World War, to which 47 states are currently signatories. The UK signed up in 1951.

6.3 Prior to the HRA 1998, which came into force in 2000, domestic courts could not directly enforce Convention rights. In order for a UK citizen to enforce their rights under the Convention, they had to bring their case to the European Court of Human Rights in Strasbourg. Now, under the HRA 1998, UK citizens can have human rights complaints heard by our domestic courts.

6.4 The HRA 1998 is a key part of the law of all the UK jurisdictions. Understanding it is essential to taking lawful decisions in a wide range of spheres, and to ensuring that individuals' rights and freedoms are respected. If you are a decision-maker to whom the HRA 1998 applies, you may need to think about its provisions when making decisions. However, what will matter in the final analysis is whether the Convention rights have been breached, not whether they have been taken into account.

6.5 This book will not address the repeated political controversy as to whether the HRA 1998 ought to be repealed or replaced with a 'Bill of

1 The Council of Europe pre-dates, and is a separate organisation to, the European Union. Britain's membership of the Council of Europe and the ECHR is not changed by its departure from the European Union.

Rights'; our focus is on the law as presently enacted by parliament. The election of the Labour government under Sir Keir Starmer as Prime Minister means any dilution of human rights protection in the near future is very unlikely.

The Human Rights Act 1998

To whom does the HRA 1998 apply?

6.6 The HRA 1998 applies to the acts of public authorities. Certain authorities will obviously be public ones, and the obligations in the HRA 1998 will apply to all their decisions. The authorities include central government departments, local authorities, prisons, the police, the probation service and NHS Trusts, as well as 'panels' or other bodies established as part of their decision-making process. Appeal bodies such as school admission and exclusion appeal panels[2] will also be 'core' public authorities, ie obliged to comply with the HRA 1998 in relation to all their decisions.

6.7 Other bodies and persons will have to comply with the HRA 1998 when they are exercising 'functions of a public nature'. These are sometimes known as 'hybrid' public authorities. For example, a housing trust, which was a registered social landlord, acted as a public authority when terminating the tenancy of an individual in social housing.[3]

6.8 Factors that may suggest that the function is 'public' in nature include whether it involves the exercise of statutory powers and whether the body exercising the function is publicly funded or is performing functions that would otherwise be performed by central or local government.[4] As such, regulatory bodies (such as the Bar Standards Board[5] and General Medical Council[6]) are often treated as public authorities. The University of Southampton was held to be a 'public authority' which was required to comply with the HRA

2 See eg *R (V) v Independent Appeal Panel for Tom Hood School* [2010] EWCA Civ 142.

3 *R (Weaver) v London & Quadrant Housing Trust* [2009] EWCA Civ 587.

4 *Aston Cantlow and Wilmcote with Billesley Parochial Church Council v Wallbank* [2003] UKHL 37 at [10].

5 *Diggins v Bar Standards Board* [2020] EWHC 467 (Admin) at [74].

6 *R (British Medical Association) v General Medical Council* [2016] EWHC 1015 (Admin).

1998 in a challenge to a decision to withdraw permission to hold a conference on campus.[7]

6.9 Housing associations can be 'hybrid' public authorities.[8] An exam board has been held to be exercising functions of a public nature.[9] So has a body conducting an independent non-statutory inquiry[10] and an independent fostering agency.[11] More specifically, a private company limited by guarantee set up by a local authority to regulate markets was held to be exercising 'functions of a public nature' in relation to its decision to reject an application by a trout farmer to participate in a programme of farmers' markets.[12]

6.10 On the other side,[13] bodies held not to be exercising functions of a public nature include a provider of temporary accommodation to former asylum-seekers that had a contract with the Home Office[14] and a rail operator when introducing a taxi permit scheme at a station.[15]

6.11 The majority of the House of Lords in *YL v Birmingham City Council*[16] held that a private care home providing care for a resident funded by a local authority was not exercising 'functions of a public nature' and so was not required to comply with the HRA 1998 in the provision of that care. *YL* is still the leading case on the approach to 'hybrid' public authorities generally. However, in its own specific context, the decision in *YL* has been overturned by parliament, most recently in section 73 of the Care Act 2014, so that most local authority funded service users are expressly entitled to the protections of the HRA 1998.[17] In the opinion of the authors, this would necessar-

7 *R (Ben-Dor) v University of Southampton* [2016] EWHC 953 (Admin).

8 *Poplar Housing & Regeneration Community Association Ltd v Donoghue* [2001] EWCA Civ 595. The decision challenged in *Poplar Housing* was to issue proceedings for possession.

9 *R (Lewisham LBC) v Assessments and Qualifications Alliance* [2013] EWHC 211 (Admin).

10 *Foreign and Commonwealth Office v Warsama* [2020] EWCA Civ 142.

11 *R (Cornerstone (North East) Adoption and Fostering Service Ltd) v Ofsted* [2020] EWHC 1679 (Admin).

12 *R (Beer (t/a Hammer Trout Farm)) v Hampshire Farmers Markets Ltd* [2003] EWCA Civ 1056.

13 For further examples on both sides, see The Hon Mr Justice C Lewis QC *Judicial Remedies in Public Law* (Sweet & Maxwell, 6th ed, 2020), at 16-020.

14 *Ali v Serco Ltd* [2019] CSIH 54.

15 *Jones v First Great Western Ltd* [2013] EWHC 1485 (Ch).

16 [2007] UKHL 27.

17 See eg *Milner v Barchester Healthcare Homes Ltd* [2022] EWHC 593 (QB), where the private care home was accepted to be a public authority for HRA 1998 purposes.

ily extend to service users who are funded by the NHS (generally through the Continuing Healthcare scheme), in order to avoid unlawful discrimination contrary to ECHR Article 14.

6.12 The authors would suggest that if a decision-maker is in doubt as to whether they are obliged to comply with the rights protected by the HRA 1998, they should proceed as if they are required to do so, not least because this will promote high standards of decision-making even if the decision is 'private' in nature.

The HRA 1998 duties

6.13 The HRA 1998 contains a number of different mechanisms to ensure that public authorities comply with Convention rights; two are likely to be particularly important for readers of this book.

6.14 First, it is unlawful for a public authority to act in a way that is incompatible with a Convention right.[18]

6.15 Second, legislation must be interpreted and applied in a way that is compatible with Convention rights, so far as it is possible to do so. This is the case regardless of whether the legislation came into force before or after the HRA 1998. The obligation is to interpret the legislation in a way that is compatible with Convention rights, unless this is plainly impossible.[19] This means that the HRA 1998 cannot be used to interpret legislation in a way that expressly contradicts a legislative provision, or in a way that departs substantially from a fundamental feature of the legislation.[20]

6.16 There is a defence potentially available to public authorities acting incompatibly with Convention rights.[21] In essence, this is that the authority was obliged, as a result of primary legislation, to breach the right. Importantly, the defence only applies if the obligation arises from *primary* legislation. That will be the case if the obligation comes directly from an Act of Parliament, or if it comes from secondary legislation[22] that has to take the form it does because of an Act of Parliament. If a provision in secondary legislation requires a decision-maker to breach someone's Convention rights, is not the necessary result of primary legislation and the statutory scheme can function without the provision, the public authority must ignore it. Otherwise,

18 HRA 1998 s6(1).

19 *R v A (No 2)* [2001] UKHL 25.

20 *Re S (children) (care order: implementation of care plan)* [2002] UKHL 10.

21 HRA 1998 s6.

22 These include, eg, regulations made by ministers.

the authority would be breaching Convention rights despite not being obliged by primary legislation to do so.[23]

6.17 It is important to emphasise that this defence will rarely be applicable: most legislation is compatible with the Convention, or it can be interpreted and applied in a compatible way. Decision-makers should therefore focus on taking decisions which do not breach Convention rights.

6.18 If it is not possible to interpret legislation to make it compatible with the Convention, certain courts have the power to issue a 'declaration of incompatibility'. This involves a formal declaration that particular provisions in legislation are incompatible with the ECHR. The incompatible legislation remains in force until it is amended by parliament.

6.19 Rather than interpreting legislation, the key task for most decision-makers will be ensuring that their decisions and actions are compatible with Convention rights. That means exercising powers and taking decisions in a way that integrates human rights considerations. In order to do that, it is necessary to understand: (1) which Convention rights, if any, apply to a particular scenario; and (2) where one or more Convention rights apply, what they require.

The Convention rights

6.20 The ECHR protects a wide range of rights and freedoms. Some of are these are contained in the main text of the Convention; others are set out in later protocols. The HRA 1998 incorporates nearly all of them, namely:

- Article 2: Right to life;
- Article 3: Prohibition of torture;
- Article 4: Prohibition of slavery and forced labour;
- Article 5: Right to liberty and security;
- Article 6: Right to a fair trial;
- Article 7: No punishment without law;
- Article 8: Right to respect for private and family life;
- Article 9: Freedom of thought, conscience and religion;
- Article 10: Freedom of expression;
- Article 11: Freedom of association;
- Article 12: Right to marry;
- Article 14: Prohibition of discrimination;

23 *RR v Secretary of State for Work and Pensions* [2019] UKSC 52.

- Article 16: Restrictions on political activity of aliens;
- Article 17: Prohibition on abuse of rights;
- Article 18: Limitation on use of restriction on rights;
- First Protocol Article 1: Protection of property;
- First Protocol Article 2: Right to education;
- First Protocol Article 3: Right to free elections; and
- Thirteenth Protocol Article 1: Abolition of the death penalty.

6.21 Several of these rights are likely to be of limited, if any, relevance to users of this book and so are not addressed in the rest of this chapter.

6.22 Before turning to the detail of particular Convention rights, it is necessary to explain some key concepts that are used in interpreting them. Understanding these will make it easier to act compatibly with the rights listed above.

Key Convention concepts

Absolute, limited and qualified rights

6.23 The Convention rights set out above can broadly be grouped into three categories: absolute, limited and qualified. These categories reflect the types of restriction, if any, that can be placed on the rights.

6.24 Absolute rights cannot be disapplied[24] in times of emergency, and interference with them cannot be justified in the public interest. They include the right to life and the prohibition on torture. Some of the rights contain exceptions to the strict prohibition: for example, the use of force in defending a person from unlawful violence, provided it is no more than absolutely necessary.

6.25 Limited rights can be restricted in specific circumstances set out in the relevant Article itself, or in circumstances which are implicit. They can be disapplied in times of emergency. They include the right to liberty, the right to a fair trial and the right to education. Any restrictions must be proportionate, a concept explained further below.

6.26 Qualified rights involve weighing up the interests of the individual and the community, and achieving a fair balance between them. The rights can be interfered with if the interference is prescribed by law, in pursuit of a specified legitimate aim and necessary in a democratic society, as explained below. This includes acting

24 'Derogated from' in the language of the Convention.

proportionately. These rights include the right to respect for family and private life.

Prescribed by/in accordance with the law

6.27 Any interference with a Convention right must be prescribed by law.[25] In short, this means that the legal basis for the interference must be sufficiently clear, certain and predictable. For example, if the security services wanted to listen in on your phone calls – which would interfere with your Article 8 ECHR right to respect for your private life – the circumstances in which it could do so, and the legal authority permitting it to eavesdrop, would have to be sufficiently clear, certain and predictable.

Legitimate aim

6.28 In order to justify interfering with a Convention right, the interference must be in pursuit of a legitimate aim. Legitimate aims that can justify interfering with a qualified right are listed in each of the relevant Articles. They include national security and public safety, the prevention of crime or disorder, the protection of public health, and the protection of the rights and freedoms of others. Identifying a legitimate aim is not usually difficult.

Necessary in a democratic society; proportionality

6.29 Interfering with a qualified Convention right must be 'necessary in a democratic society'. This requirement is generally divided into three parts. The most important part is proportionality, which is a key concept in understanding qualified rights. Broadly speaking, the test of proportionality is used to decide whether a decision which interferes with or limits certain rights can be justified. The test is divided into the following four questions, which frequently overlap in practice:[26]

(1) Is the objective behind the interference sufficiently important to justify limiting a fundamental right?
(2) Are the measures which have been designed to meet the objective rationally connected to it?

25 An alternative expression is 'in accordance with law'.
26 *Bank Mellat v HM Treasury* [2013] UKSC 39.

(3) Do the measures go no further than necessary to accomplish the objective?
(4) Do they strike a fair balance between the rights of the individual and the interests of the community?

6.30 Whether or not a decision is proportionate is a very fact-specific issue. Factors to bear in mind include:

(1) The extent of the interference with the right. The greater the interference, the more compelling the reasons for it will have to be. Restrictions will not be proportionate if, in effect, they reduce the right to such an extent as to extinguish it.
(2) The nature of the right or issue. For example, particularly strong reasons will be necessary to show that a measure which is discriminatory on grounds of race, sex or disability (so called 'suspect grounds') is proportionate.[27] Similarly, it may be more difficult to justify interfering with the right to privacy than with property rights.
(3) Whether a less intrusive or restrictive measure could be used.

6.31 The other two requirements of an interference being 'necessary in a democratic society' are that it relates to a 'pressing social need', and that relevant and sufficient reasons are given for the interference.

Positive obligations

6.32 Generally, the Convention imposes negative obligations on public authorities: ie it prevents them from interfering with individuals' rights. In certain cases, it also imposes positive obligations: active steps a public authority must take in order to avoid Convention rights being breached. However, the courts have been reluctant to impose positive obligations that involve financial commitments for public bodies, other than where the circumstances would result in inhuman or degrading treatment contrary to Article 3 ECHR.[28]

Key ECHR Articles

6.33 We address below some of the Articles of the ECHR which are most likely to be relevant to decision-makers.

27 *R (SC) v Secretary of State for Work and Pensions* [2021] UKSC 26.
28 See here *Anufrijeva v Southwark LBC* [2003] EWCA Civ 1406.

Article 6: Right to a fair trial

6.34 Article 6 ensures the fundamental right to a fair trial or hearing. It applies most obviously in criminal trials.

6.35 Outside of the criminal context, Article 6 is engaged in decisions that involve 'the determination of . . . civil rights and obligations'. Whether this test is met is not always straightforward to decide. The application of Article 6 to decisions around social security and welfare benefits, for example, has been particularly difficult to resolve.[29] In summary, the test is whether:

- there is a genuine and serious dispute relating to a civil right or obligation recognised in domestic law, which can include whether the right exists as well as its scope and exercise; and
- the proceedings are decisive for the rights and obligations, ie they determine them.

6.36 This will be the case where, for example, an individual is being sued for negligence, or a family court is deciding a contact dispute between parents. Article 6 has also been held to apply to the determination of planning disputes,[30] licensing decisions (such as for the sale of alcohol[31]), regulatory decisions around a person's right to practise a profession[32] and anti-social behaviour orders.[33]

6.37 Cases in which Article 6 has been found not to be engaged include tax decisions,[34] the right to stand for election,[35] and the admission or exclusion decisions of schools.[36]

6.38 Where it applies, Article 6(1) guarantees a 'fair and public hearing within a reasonable time by an independent and impartial tribunal established by law'. This implies a right to effective access to a court or tribunal (understood broadly), which in some cases may require the state to provide legal aid. The right to a public hearing means that any departure from that position needs to be carefully considered and objectively justified.[37]

29 See eg *Poshteh v Kensington and Chelsea RBLC* [2017] UKSC 36.

30 *Bryan v United Kingdom* (App No A/335-A) (1996) 21 EHRR 342, ECtHR.

31 *Tre Traktorer AB v Sweden* (App No A/159) (1991) 13 EHRR 309, ECtHR.

32 *Le Compte v Belgium* (App No A/43) (1982) 4 EHRR 1, ECtHR.

33 *R (McCann) v Manchester Crown Court* [2002] UKHL 39.

34 *Ferrazzini v Italy* (App No 44759/98) (2002) 34 EHRR 45, ECtHR.

35 *Pierre-Bloch v France* (App No 24194/94) (1998) 26 EHRR 202, ECtHR.

36 *R v Richmond LBC Appeal Committee ex p JC (a child)* [2001] ELR 21, CA; *R (B (a child)) v Alperton Community School Head Teacher and Governing Body* [2001] EWHC Admin 229.

37 *Miller v General Medical Council* [2013] EWHC 1934 (Admin).

6.39 The following factors are relevant to whether a tribunal is independent:[38]

- how its members are appointed;
- the duration of their term of office;
- the existence of safeguards against outside pressures; and
- whether the body appears independent.

6.40 If a decision-making body is not sufficiently independent and impartial, the overall process may still be compliant with Article 6 provided that an appeal or review by a tribunal which does meet the standards of Article 6 is available.

6.41 Article 6(1) includes the following exceptions to the requirement to hold a public hearing:

> . . . the press and the public may be excluded from all or part of the trial in the interests of morals, public order or national security in a democratic society, where the interests of juveniles so require, or to the extent strictly necessary in the opinion of the court in special circumstances where publicity would prejudice the interests of justice.

6.42 In cases involving children, private hearings will be the norm. In other scenarios, exceptions to the requirement for a public hearing must be applied restrictively:[39] that is, they should go no further than is necessary to protect the relevant interest (such as the interests of justice). One way to do this is to hold only certain parts of a hearing in private where it is necessary to do so. Another way is to anonymise parties or witnesses. In some cases a person may waive their right to their hearing being held in public, though any such waiver must be unequivocal.[40] See further chapter 3 at para 3.9 onwards on the question of private hearings generally.

6.43 Whether a hearing has been held and a decision reached in a reasonable time will depend on the circumstances. Particularly relevant factors will include the complexity of the case, the conduct of the applicant, the conduct of the relevant authorities and the significance of what is being decided to the applicant.[41]

6.44 In order for a hearing to be fair, there must be equality of arms between the parties (see paras 3.39–3.43 above). This requires that each party be given a reasonable opportunity to present its case and

38 *Campbell v United Kingdom* (App No A/80) (1985) 7 EHRR 165, ECtHR.

39 *Dienett v France* (App No A/315-B) (1996) 21 EHRR 554, ECtHR.

40 *Hakansson v Sweden* (App No A/171) (1991) 13 EHRR 1, ECtHR.

41 *Gast v Germany* (App No 29357/95) (2001) 33 EHRR 37, ECtHR.

take part in proceedings, and to do so under conditions which do not give one party a substantial advantage over the other.[42]

6.45 Article 6 also requires a court or tribunal to give reasons for its judgment. The extent of the detail required in giving reasons will depend on the circumstances: there is no requirement to cover every argument, but the essential issues have to be addressed. Provided a decision-maker complies with its common law duty to give reasons (see chapter 4 at para 4.107 onwards), it should not be in breach of Article 6.[43]

Qualified rights

Article 8: Private and family life

6.46 Article 8 protects several related rights: respect for a person's private life, family life, home and correspondence. It has a broad scope. For example, respect for private life includes the protection of personal data, freedom from unjustified press intrusion or state surveillance, as well as gender, sexual and personal autonomy. It also protects the physical and psychological integrity of disabled people and their ability to function socially.[44]

6.47 Article 8 requires public authorities to avoid interfering with the rights it protects, unless the interference can be justified. It includes a number of positive obligations. It may also require the decision to be subject to procedural safeguards.[45] The question is whether, having regard to the particular circumstances of the case and the nature of the decisions to be taken, those affected have been involved in the decision-making process, seen as a whole, to a degree sufficient to provide them with the requisite protection of their interests.[46]

6.48 Article 8 is a qualified right. This means that interferences with it can be justified, provided the interference is in accordance with the law and necessary in a democratic society for one of the aims listed in Article 8(2), which involves acting proportionately (see para 6.29 onwards above). The aims include national security, public safety,

42 *Bulut v Austria* (App No 17358/90) (1997) 24 EHRR 84, ECtHR.

43 *English v Emery Reimbold & Strick Ltd* [2002] EWCA Civ 605.

44 *R (Razgar) v Secretary of State for the Home Department (No 2)* [2004] UKHL 27; *Pretty v United Kingdom* (App No 2346/02) (2002) 35 EHRR 1, ECtHR.

45 See eg *McCann v United Kingdom* (App No 19009/04) (2008) 47 EHRR 40, ECtHR.

46 *R (B) v Chief Constable of Derbyshire* [2011] EWHC 2362 (Admin) at [48].

economic well-being, the protection of health or morals, and the protection of the rights and freedoms of others.

Article 9: Freedom of thought, conscience and religion

6.49 Article 9 protects freedom of thought, conscience and religion.

6.50 The rights protected by Article 9 include the right to change one's religion or belief, and to manifest it in practice and observance, in public and in private. Non-religious beliefs protected by Article 9 include pacifism.[47] The right to hold a belief is absolute, while the right to manifest one is qualified.[48]

6.51 In order for there to be an interference with a manifestation, there must be more than an association between the religion or belief and the manifestation; they must be intimately linked.[49]

6.52 As with Article 8, Article 9(2) enables certain interferences with the rights it protects to be justified.[50]

Article 10: Freedom of expression

6.53 Article 10 protects the right to freedom of expression. This includes the right to hold opinions and to receive and impart information and ideas without interference by a public authority.

6.54 The types of expression protected by Article 10 are broad. They include political, artistic and commercial expression. Speech that offends, shocks or disturbs is included, within limits: for example, it does not protect Holocaust denial.

6.55 Interferences with Article 10 can be justified provided that they are in accordance with Article 10(2).[51] For example, the refusal to allow publication of an advert on a bus which stated 'NOT GAY! EX-GAY, POST-GAY AND PROUD, GET OVER IT' was found to

47 *Arrowsmith v United Kingdom* (App No 7050/75) (1981) 3 EHRR 218, ECtHR.

48 *R (Williamson) v Secretary of State for Education and Employment* [2005] UKHL 15 at [16].

49 For example, a 16-year-old school pupil's desire to wear a 'purity' ring as a symbol of her commitment to celibacy before marriage was not a manifestation of her Christian faith: *R (Playfoot) v Millais School Governors* [2007] EWHC 1698 (Admin). By contrast, the desire of an orthodox Hindu to be cremated on an open-air funeral pyre was a manifestation of his religious beliefs, as it was sufficiently close to the core of one strand of orthodox Hinduism: *R (Ghai) v Newcastle City Council* [2010] EWCA Civ 59 at [101].

50 See eg *Eweida v United Kingdom* (App No 48420/10) [2013] IRLR 231, ECtHR and *R (Begum) v Denbigh High School Governors* [2006] UKHL 15.

51 Note that Article 10 also expressly permits the licensing of broadcasting, television and cinema.

be necessary and proportionate having regard to the rights of gay people under Article 8, the need to avoid causing widespread offence to the public, and the transport operator's duties under the Equality Act 2010.[52]

Article 14: Discrimination

6.56 Article 14 prohibits discrimination that relates to the rights and freedoms set out elsewhere in the ECHR. It requires Convention rights to be secured without discrimination on any ground. Article 14 contains an illustrative and non-exhaustive list of such grounds. They include sex, race, colour, language, religion, political or other opinion, national or social origin, association with a national minority, property, birth or 'other status'. 'Other status' has been held to include disability (including different types and levels of impairment),[53] military rank,[54] marital status,[55] place of residence[56] and immigration status.[57]

6.57 Article 14 does not, therefore, provide a free-standing prohibition on discrimination. The alleged discrimination has to be connected to another Convention right.

6.58 This does not mean that Article 14 only applies to cases where there has been an arguable breach of another Convention right; it applies where Convention rights are engaged. This includes rights that a public authority has decided to provide and that are additional to those which would otherwise be available.[58] For example, the right to respect for private and family life in Article 8 does not provide the right to adopt a child, but if legislation is introduced to enable adoption, it must do so in a non-discriminatory way.[59]

6.59 Discrimination occurs under Article 14 where people in comparable situations are treated differently and there is no objective or reasonable justification for the difference. It also occurs where, without proper justification, people are treated similarly to those in a

52 *R (Core Issues Trust) v Transport for London* [2014] EWCA Civ 34. See also *R (Ben-Dor) v University of Southampton* [2016] EWHC 953 (Admin).

53 *Mathieson v Secretary of State for Work and Pensions* [2015] UKSC 47.

54 *Engel v Netherlands* (App No A/22) (1979–80) 1 EHRR 647, ECtHR.

55 *Sahin v Germany* (App No 30943/96) (2003) 36 EHRR 43, ECtHR.

56 *Darby v Sweden* (App No A/187) (1991) 13 EHRR 774, ECtHR.

57 *Bah v United Kingdom* (App No 56328/07) (2012) 54 EHRR 21, ECtHR.

58 *Stec v United Kingdom (admissibility)* (App No 65731/01) (2005) 41 EHRR SE18, ECtHR.

59 *EB v France* (App No 43546/02) (2008) 47 EHRR 21, ECtHR.

different situation when they should have been treated differently.[60] The test for identifying whether a proper justification exists can vary, but it usually depends on whether what is being done has a legitimate aim, and whether there is a reasonable relationship of proportionality between the aim and the means used to achieve it.

6.60 Differential treatment on certain grounds – sometimes referred to as 'suspect' grounds – requires particularly weighty and convincing reasons to be justified. These include sex[61] and race.[62] By contrast, where the difference in treatment relates to strategic social or economic policy, greater leeway will generally be given to public authorities when scrutinising their justifications for different treatment.[63]

Article 1 Protocol 1

6.61 Article 1 of Protocol 1 (A1P1) is about the protection of property. It provides that every natural or legal person is entitled to the peaceful enjoyment of their possessions, and that no one shall be deprived of their possessions except in the public interest and subject to the conditions provided by law and by the general principles of international law. 'Possessions' has a broad meaning and extends beyond physical property. It includes interests in land, shares, intellectual property rights and certain state benefits. A1P1 also contains a positive obligation on the state, in certain cases, to take steps to protect possessions.[64]

6.62 A1P1 distinguishes between three progressively intrusive cases, which will generally be increasingly difficult to justify: interfering with possessions; controlling possessions; and depriving a person of them.

6.63 A1P1 rights are subject to an express limitation: the right of a state to enforce the law it considers necessary to control the use of property in the general interest, or to ensure the payment of taxes or other contributions or penalties. The ability to interfere with or control the use of property 'in the general interest' has a broad scope, rather than being limited to specified aims. In order to be justified, an interference with A1P1 rights must be in accordance with

60 *Thlimmenos v Greece* (App No 34369/97) (2001) 31 EHRR 15, ECtHR.

61 *Van Raalte v Netherlands* (App No 20060/92) (1997) 24 EHRR 503, ECtHR.

62 *DH v Czech Republic* (App No 57325/00) (2008) 47 EHRR 3, ECtHR.

63 See *R (SC) v Secretary of State for Work and Pensions* [2021] UKSC 26 for detailed consideration of the approach to justification under Article 14.

64 See eg *Oneryildiz v Turkey (No 2)* (App No 48939/99) (2005) 41 EHRR 20, ECtHR.

conditions provided by law, and achieve a fair balance between the interests of the community and the property rights of the persons in question. This requires a reasonable relationship of proportionality between the aim and the means used to achieve it.

Demonstrating compliance with the Human Rights Act 1998

6.64 An important issue for decision-makers is how best to demonstrate that their decisions comply with the HRA 1998.

6.65 Identifying the issues and considering the right questions are key first steps. In the context of the HRA 1998, it is important to identify which, if any, Convention rights are engaged in order to ensure the right questions are asked.

6.66 Next, decision-makers should ensure that they have adequate evidence to resolve the issues and answer the relevant questions. Complying with the HRA 1998 does not require any special form of evidence; nor does a decision need to be in any particular format to be HRA 1998-compliant. The evidence should, however, be sufficiently clear and compelling to demonstrate compliance with fundamental rights, and relevant to the particular requirements of Convention rights, in particular when seeking to justify a restriction or interference with a limited or qualified right.

6.67 As for the point at which to undertake these tasks, there are two broad approaches. Under the first, the decision-maker reaches their decision and then considers whether it breaches the HRA 1998, perhaps modifying it accordingly. This effectively treats human rights issues as an 'add-on' to the substance of a decision. Under the second, the decision-maker identifies human rights issues at the outset, and integrates them into the decision-making process.

6.68 Both of these approaches can lead to lawful results. There is no set rule requiring one over the other, and in many cases the outcome will be the same. Nonetheless, we suggest adopting the second one. This should not be unduly onerous, as human rights issues simply will not arise in many areas of decision-making. Where they do, incorporating them into the decision-making process has a key advantage: helping to ensure that decision-makers ask themselves the right questions and obtain relevant evidence. We suggest that taking this approach is likely to lead to better quality decisions, and to fewer examples of individuals' rights being breached.

Complying with the Human Rights Act 1998: Checklist

6.69 The checklist below is intended to support decision-makers to make sure that their decisions are compliant with the key ECHR rights discussed above. It is of course not a substitute for legal advice in a particular case.

Checklist

- Does your decision have to comply with the Human Rights Act 1998? If you are a public body, the answer is yes.
- Are anyone's Convention rights relevant to the decision you are considering?
- If a Convention right is relevant, could the decision you are considering taking interfere with or restrict the right?
- If the decision would involve an interference or restriction, could it be permissible? Consider whether the right is an absolute, limited or qualified one. If it is absolute, your decision cannot interfere with or restrict it.
- If the right is limited or qualified, and interfering with or restricting it could in principle be justified, would it be proportionate to do so? This involves considering:
  - whether your objective is sufficiently important to justify limiting a fundamental right;
  - whether the measures you are considering in order to meet your objective are rationally connected to it;
  - whether the measures go further than necessary to accomplish your objective; and
  - whether they strike a fair balance between the rights of the individual and the interests of the community.
- At each stage of the decision-making process – and in particular if you are considering interfering with or restricting someone's Convention rights – do you have enough evidence to support your conclusion?

Remedies

6.70 Under section 8 of the HRA 1998, a court is able to grant such relief or remedy, or make such order, within its powers as it considers just and appropriate where it identifies a breach of a Convention right. This can include awarding damages.

6.71 In deciding whether to award damages, and if so how much to award, the court must take into account the principles applied by the European Court of Human Rights in relation to the award of compensation under Article 41 ECHR. This requires consideration of whether damages are needed to provide 'just satisfaction' to the claimant. Any pecuniary loss arising from the Convention breach will usually be compensated under this approach. Damages can also be awarded for non-pecuniary loss, including distress, but the sums involved in such awards tend to be relatively modest. There are, however, exceptions to this, for example, lengthy periods of unlawful detention of a disabled person where the deprivation of liberty was more than merely 'technical' (for example, a person kept in a care home against their wishes who could have returned home) can result in a very substantial damages award.

CHAPTER 7

Remedies

7.1 Where a party is aggrieved by a decision, there are a number of remedies that may be available. Generally, these remedies require there to be evidence of procedural errors by the decision-maker. However, it can also be possible to challenge the substantive outcome, generally on grounds that it is 'irrational' or because it breaches human rights or equality standards.

7.2 This chapter provides some basic information about complaining to an ombudsman, and bringing court proceedings for judicial review to challenge decisions of public bodies.

What is an ombudsman?

7.3 An ombudsman is a body which deals with unresolved complaints about other organisations. Before going to an ombudsman, it is generally necessary first to use the relevant body's own complaints procedure.

7.4 Public sector ombudsman services typically consider complaints of maladministration by public bodies. This includes consideration of problems such as delay, unfairness, incompetence and impropriety. Unlike going to court, the ombudsman service is completely free. There are also ombudsmen in the private sector, for example, the Legal Ombudsman, the Rail Ombudsman and the Energy Ombudsman. The Legal Ombudsman states that: 'We decide each case based on what was reasonable in those circumstances.'[1]

Which ombudsman is appropriate?

7.5 There is a range of different ombudsman services, which deal with different types of public and private bodies.[2] The main public sector ombudsman schemes are:

- the Parliamentary and Health Service Ombudsman (for complaints about government departments and the NHS);[3] and
- the Local Government and Social Care Ombudsman (for complaints against local authorities).[4]

1 www.legalombudsman.org.uk/how-we-work/

2 www.citizensadvice.org.uk/consumer/get-more-help/how-to-use-an-ombudsman-in-england/

3 www.ombudsman.org.uk/about-us/contact-us/

4 www.lgo.org.uk/

What is the procedure and what are the time limits?

7.6 Every ombudsman has its own procedure, generally explained on the ombudsman's website. For example, it is common to have to fill out a complaint form. It is also common for the ombudsman to require a complainant to have completed any internal complaints procedures available. Ombudsmen often will not investigate if the issue has been, or perhaps even could have been, the subject of legal proceedings.

7.7 Generally, matters must be raised with the ombudsman within 12 months of the complainant becoming aware of the subject-matter of the complaint. It will be important to check the specific time requirements for the relevant ombudsman as soon as the potential need to make a complaint is identified.

What can the ombudsman do?

7.8 If the ombudsman decides to investigate the issue, the relevant body is required to co-operate with the investigation. This may involve sharing relevant documentation, facilitating site visits and making representations to the ombudsman. In simple cases, the investigation may take a few weeks. However, complex cases can take significantly longer, up to a year or even longer in the most complex cases.

7.9 Once the investigation is complete, the ombudsman will make a recommendation. The recommendation could be for an apology, the payment of a certain amount of compensation (not normally a very large sum) and/or a change in practice so that the problem does not occur in the future. Whether the body is required to comply with the recommendation will depend on the rules governing the specific ombudsman scheme. Public bodies generally comply with the recommendations of the ombudsman, but they are not required to do so.

When is judicial review appropriate?

7.10 The decision of a public body can be challenged in the court through judicial review (see para 7.14 onwards below) if it contains an error of law.

7.11 Aggrieved parties will sometimes believe that they are required to use the complaints process (including the ombudsman) before embarking on a claim for judicial review. This is wrong; in almost every case, a complaint to the ombudsman or an application for judicial review should be seen as alternative options. There are a number of reasons for this, but the most obvious is that if a complainant uses the complaints process, it is almost certain that they will then be out of time to challenge the original decision by way of judicial review (see further para 7.16 onwards below on the requirement for 'promptness' in judicial review).

7.12 Where the primary concern with the public body's decision lies in the legal approach, normally this is a matter best considered by the courts rather than the ombudsman. Further, where the complaint concerns an ongoing matter that is serious and requires resolution urgently, judicial review will often be the most appropriate way forward. For example, if the problem lies in a local authority not providing a disabled child with necessary support in breach of its statutory duties, the fastest way to resolve the problem is likely to be an urgent application for judicial review. However, there is a risk that the Administrative Court may refuse permission to apply for judicial review if the judge considers that the complaints process should have been used.

7.13 The test to be applied here is whether there is an alternative remedy to judicial review that would be convenient and effective.[5] The burden will be on the claimant to show why a potentially available alternative remedy (such as the complaints process/ombudsman) could not be used.

Judicial review

What is judicial review?

7.14 Judicial review is the key mechanism for challenging the decision of a public body in the courts. As the name indicates, in an application for judicial review an Administrative Court judge will review the relevant decision to determine whether it is legally flawed. Importantly, the judge cannot re-make the decision just because they disagree with it; their role is to decide whether the existing decision contains an error of law.[6] This means that, normally, the judge is primarily concerned with the process which led to the decision rather than the decision itself.

7.15 However, decisions can also be challenged in substance, generally on grounds that they are irrational, in the sense of being outside the range of decisions reasonably open to the decision-maker. A further

5 *Kay v Lambeth LBC* [2006] UKHL 10 at [30] per Lord Bingham.

6 See chapter 4 for an explanation of the main types of error of law.

substantive challenge may be that the decision breaches the Human Rights Act 1998 or the Equality Act 2010 (albeit that Equality Act 2010 claims will usually go to the county court).[7]

When must the claim be brought?

7.16 A claim for judicial review must be brought promptly, and not later than three months after the grounds to make the claim first arose.[8] In some cases, such as planning cases, there are shorter time limits. The court has a discretion to extend time, but the rules on this make it increasingly difficult for claimants to obtain such an extension.

7.17 It is possible for claimants to bring their judicial review claim both too early and too late. It will be said that the claim is too early if a final decision has not been taken, or if an internal appeals process has not been used (see discussion on this at paras 7.24–7.25 below). It will be said that the claim is too late if it has not been issued promptly after the final decision (or, more technically, after the date on which the grounds of the claim first arose). It is immediately obvious that there are real pitfalls in terms of timing for inexperienced claimants who are contemplating a claim for judicial review.

7.18 As such, anyone considering challenging a decision by way of judicial review should get specialist legal advice as soon as possible, in particular to minimise the risk of being out of time (if permission to apply for judicial review is refused because the claim is premature, it can at least potentially be issued again at the correct time, albeit that the claimant will have wasted costs in bringing the premature claim). It is also important to recognise that time is not extended because the claimant is trying to use an alternative remedy, such as a complaints process/ombudsman. Nor can time be extended by agreement, although potential defendants can be asked to agree to take a new decision (and thereby start time running again) if the parties wish to negotiate pre-issue.

What can be challenged?

7.19 Often it is easy to identify the relevant decision under challenge. For example, a local authority may have made a decision to cut the

7 See *R (Adath Yisroel Burial Society) v HM Senior Coroner for Inner North London* [2018] EWHC 969 (Admin) at [136] for discussion of when it may be appropriate for an Equality Act 2010 claim to proceed by way of judicial review.

8 Civil Procedure Rules 54.5.

number of hours in someone's care plan. However, it is also possible to challenge actions and failures to act. Moreover, these can be treated as 'ongoing' rather than a one-off decision. This means that a local authority could be challenged for its ongoing failure (which may have lasted for years) to undertake a care needs assessment or for failing to provide the care specified in a person's care plan.

7.20 It is also possible to challenge policies and certain types of legislation in some circumstances. These challenges also need to be brought promptly, by reference to when the claimant was first affected by the policy or law. In these more complex cases, it is particularly important to get specialist legal advice as soon as possible, to minimise the risk of being too late to bring the claim.

Who can bring a claim for judicial review?

7.21 The person bringing a claim for judicial review, the claimant, must have 'standing' to do so. This means that they must have 'sufficient interest' in the matter to which the claim relates. For example, if a professional regulator decides to 'strike off' one of its members, clearly that person has sufficient interest in the decision to challenge it. However, it is doubtful that another unconnected member would have the right to do so.

7.22 Most of the time it will be obvious that the person who wants to challenge a decision has standing to do so, but in the rare case where this is likely to be in issue, specialist advice will be needed as soon as possible.

Who can a claim for judicial review be brought against?

7.23 The general principle is that a claim for judicial review may be brought against any body exercising a 'public function'.[9] This means that a public body (such as a local authority, prison, NHS Trust, school, or regulator) can be challenged by way of judicial review when it is acting in its 'public' capacity.

Do other appeals mechanisms need to be exhausted first?

7.24 Judicial review is supposed to be a remedy of last resort. This means that a judge will not permit a claim for judicial review to proceed if

9 *R v Panel on Take-overs and Mergers ex p Datafin plc* [1987] QB 815, CA.

there are 'alternative remedies' available. In practice, this often means that all internal appeal procedures must be used before a claim for judicial review can be brought.

7.25 However, the question is whether an alternative remedy is convenient and effective.[10] There may be rare cases where the issue is so urgent, and the appeal process is not sufficiently prompt, such that a claimant could persuade an Administrative Court judge to hear an application for judicial review against the original decision. Again, specialist advice will be needed as soon as possible about when and whether it is the right time to proceed to judicial review.

What is the procedure?

7.26 Broadly speaking, there are two stages to a claim for judicial review. The first stage is known as the 'permission stage'. A judge will consider the claim and the public body's initial defence on the papers. If the judge thinks the claim is 'arguable' and there are no procedural bars (for example, delay or a lack of standing), permission to proceed to the next stage will be granted. If not, permission is refused.

7.27 The second stage is known as the 'substantive hearing'. At this time, a hearing (normally somewhere between half a day and two days) will be held. In very simple or urgent cases, the judge may make their decision at the end of the hearing. However, normally the decision is sent in writing several weeks after the hearing.

7.28 For further information about the court procedure when bringing a claim for judicial review, see the *Administrative Court Judicial Review Guide 2023*.[11]

What can the judge be asked to do?

7.29 If the judge agrees with the claimant that there is an error of law in the decision, they can provide a remedy. However, all remedies are discretionary so the judge could formally recognise the error but take no further action. Further, relief must be refused if the defendant can show that it is highly likely that the outcome for the applicant would have been the same if the error had not been made.[12]

10 See footnote 5 above.

11 Courts and Tribunals Judiciary (2023), available at www.judiciary.uk/courts-and-tribunals/high-court/administrative-court/administrative-court-judicial-review-guide-2022/

12 Senior Courts Act 1981 s31(2A). This requirement can be avoided in cases of exceptional public interest: see subsection 2B.

7.30 In the majority of successful claims for judicial review, the judge sets aside the decision and the matter is then referred back to the original decision-maker to re-make the decision. This is known as a 'quashing order'. For example, in a planning case the judge could set aside a grant of planning permission. It will then be open to the local authority to reconsider the matter. There is nothing to stop the local authority then granting the planning permission again, but this time avoiding the procedural error that made the previous decision unlawful.

7.31 The main available remedies in a claim for judicial review are outlined below.

Declaration

7.32 The court makes a formal declaration that the decision contains an error of law. The court may also make a declaration as to the correct construction of a statutory provision or the nature of a common law right.

Quashing order

7.33 A quashing order means that the judge quashes (or 'sets aside') the decision.

Mandatory order

7.34 A mandatory order requires the public body to do something. This remedy is relatively rare, generally being granted when there is only one lawful action the public body can take.

Prohibiting order

7.35 A prohibiting order prohibits the public body from doing something. This remedy is also relatively rare.

Injunction

7.36 An injunction requires a public body to do or not to do something. This remedy is normally only relied on at an interim stage if the claimant requires the public body to do something urgently while the claim is progressing.

Damages

7.37 Damages may be claimed in very limited circumstances, for example, when a breach of a right established by the European Convention on

Human Rights is alleged (see chapter 6, Complying with the Human Rights Act 1998).

A word of warning

7.38 Judicial review is a highly specialist area of law. Anyone seriously considering a claim for judicial review is therefore strongly advised to seek professional legal advice. In some cases, legal aid will be available.

7.39 It is also important to note that normally (there are some exceptions to this) the losing party in a claim for judicial review is obliged to pay the other side's legal costs. This means that bringing an unsuccessful claim for judicial review can have serious financial implications. The costs involved in judicial review proceedings are likely to run into tens of thousands of pounds, or even more. Where a claimant cannot properly be expected to meet those costs, it is possible to apply for a 'costs capping order', but, again, specialist advice will be required on this issue. This is why many claims for judicial review, particularly in the social welfare context, will be funded via legal aid.

Index